THE BOOK MINE

Rajula and the Web of Danger

Deepa Agarwal has written around 50 books for children and adults. *Caravan to Tibet* (Penguin/Puffin, 2007), selected for the IBBY Honour List 2008 as the best book from India, and a translation of the famous Hindi classic *Chandrakanta* (Penguin/Puffin, 2008) are two of her recent titles. Deepa has won the NCERT National Award for her picture book, *Ashok's New Friends* (Children's Book Trust). Five of her books have been listed in the White Raven Catalogue brought out by the IYL, Munich.

DEEPA AGARWAL

Rajula and the Web of Danger

Introduction by

PRASOON JOSHI

hachette INDIA

First published in 2012 by Hachette India
(Registered name: Hachette Book Publishing India Pvt. Ltd)
An Hachette UK company
www.hachetteindia.com

SRD

ISBN 978-93-50093-31-3

Hachette Book Publishing India Pvt Ltd,
4th & 5th Floors, Corporate Centre;
Plot No. 94, Sector 44; Gurgaon 122003, India

Typeset in Goudy Old Style 11.5/15.5 by
Eleven Arts, New Delhi
Printed and bound in India by
Manipal Technologies Limited, Manipal

MIX
Paper from responsible sources
FSC™ C043100

{Contents}

Introduction

Growing up in the lap of the Himalayas in the land referred to as 'Dev Bhoomi' (Uttarakhand) has left an imprint on my soul. The memories of sitting huddled around a makeshift fire, eating *bhune huye bhatt* (roasted soya bean) and listening to stories narrated by my grandmother, or an elderly relative, are as fresh as if they happened yesterday.

These stories—the folk tales and the folk songs—entered so effortlessly into my stream of consciousness that they became a defining element shaping my world as I grew up.

After all, a folk tale has a significant role, both in distilling ancient wisdom and influencing current character. Through these stories one can relate to the lives of common people and the manner in which they dealt with ordinary and extraordinary circumstances. They oscillate between the ironic and the lyrical, enveloping tales of valour, of true love, of strength, of goodness, brotherhood and a sense of community, of Gods with human leanings, and of the limitations of humans and their sheer tenacity to overcome them.

Adding to these inherent values is the sheer artistic richness of the folk stories of Kumaon and Garhwal. Be it those of Golu, Gangnath, Narsingh and Ghana, Purukh Pant or the fabulous tales of Haru–Sem, Kalsem and Churmal Airi . . . they are all incredible. In fact, many of these tales in the form of ballads are sung in diverse melodies such as Nyoli, Jaagar Geet, Chapheli, Chaiti, Malushahi, Ramol, Jhoda, Chanchari, Hudkia Baul and more.

The sheer power of these folk tales lies in the wondrous co-existence of fantasy with reality. It shows you the mirror of existing reality, but it also reflects the limitless sky of possibility in the background.

Rajula–Malushahi is one such charming folk tale of Kumaon. It is a romantic narrative, the story of a king (Malushahi), and the daughter (Rajula) of a trader. The canvas is big, painted on with a myriad experiences and umpteen human emotions, including those about parental duty, honour and personal love. The mysteries and the mythological elements go hand in hand with the traditions and the limitations of the societal and geographical conditions. It's one of those love ballads that you will find alive and sung in many parts of Uttarakhand.

What shines through this epic ballad is the multi-ethnic character of life in Kumaon. Malushahi is from a Khasa family; his beloved is from the tribe of Shaukas. Rajula is promised in marriage to a Tibetan ruler for economic and political gain. The story is woven around the different challenges the two divinely ordained lovers face before they can finally get together. The playing out of ethnic characteristics and practices is fascinating. Add to it the vivid descriptions of the Himalayan land, the references to the local gods and goddesses—Lord Baghnath (Bageshwar), Chitrashila Devi; the village fairs; the local cuisine such as *alu gutak*; musical instruments such as the flute and folk dances like the *jhoda*... and you get a colourful, eventful, unputdownable tale.

The more striking feature to mind is, however, the central and very active role that Rajula plays. She is an exceptionally smart and spirited heroine, a young woman with a free-thinking mind and the initiative to act on it. And that, in a way, is a tribute to and reflection of the women of Pahad, who are hardworking, resilient, equally adept at tending the field and keeping the home fires burning, and in many ways less constrained than their counterparts in other parts of the country. In fact, Rajula stands in marked contrast to many female protagonists from other parts of the country, whose virtues veer towards docility and conformity rather than initiative and daring.

And this portrayal is extremely important.

You see, folk tales are not just stories. They are capsules of culture. They contain the traditions, the morality, the challenges and the wisdom of not one but many a generation. You can get the feel of a particular region, its people, their ideas, and their concerns by listening to the folk tales of the area. For no matter how powerful or how insignificant or wealthy or disadvantaged, we are all faced with challenges and obstacles to overcome. Throughout generations the ways to address these have been honed and woven in the form of folk stories that are easy to understand and relate to.

And like a river stone that becomes smooth with years of the water flowing on it, these stories, too, over generations, continue to get more refined without losing their inherent character. The folk culture of a region is its most natural character, its very soul.

I congratulate Deepa Agarwal for keeping the soul of the Kumaon region alive by retelling and bringing to your hands this beautiful tale of Rajula and Malushahi.

Prasoon Joshi
October 2011

1

The Dream

The voice crept into Rajula's ears, breaking the spell—a woman's voice. She struggled to free herself from it, like a mountain trout trying to unhook itself from a fisherman's line. Even though it seemed comfortingly familiar, it was dragging her away from the enchantment that gripped her.

The bright eyes of the young man before her began to grow fuzzy as the voice turned louder. The touch of his hands became fainter and fainter. She strove to hold on with all her might, the way a climber teetering at the edge of a mountain clutches at a frail clump of grass. Rajula knew he was going to say something wonderful next; his mouth was already shaping the words.

A woman's voice crying, 'Rajula! Rajula!' interposed, however, shattering the spell. Without any warning, a misty darkness swallowed him. Rajula was left with nothing but the frantic drumbeat of her heart.

When she realized that she was in her own room and it was her mother calling out to her, she groaned in frustration.

'Rajula! Rajula? Are you still sleeping, child?'

Rajula squeezed her eyes shut defiantly and hugged her fleecy blanket close. She could have screamed. The dream had been so enthralling, so real. If only Ija had not interrupted it!

'Rajula! What's wrong with you? Do you want me to pull you out of bed?' She could sense that Ija was standing close by. Her mother scent, a combination of the rose attar she liked to use and the tang of spices from cooking, was very strong.

Exasperated, Rajula sat up with a jerk. Startled, Ija took a couple of hasty steps backward. Rajula couldn't help giggling at the sight of her face—fine brows arching high into her broad forehead, her eyes round with surprise.

Ija shook her head, tried to cover up her smile with a frown. 'Girl! What am I to do with you? The sun has climbed high above the mountains and you're still in bed.'

'Oh, Ija! I had such a wonderful dream! Why did you wake me up?'

Ganguli, Rajula's mother, glowered in earnest now. But her voice was gentle as she said, 'This is no time to dream. Get ready at once. Don't you remember that we leave for the lowlands today? Your father has been asking for you over and over again.' Gloom darkened her face as she continued, 'And . . . you have to change your ways. Get up in time in the morning, behave more decorously. You're not a child any longer. Don't forget that you have been promised in marriage to the Tibetan ruler, Rikhyepal.'

An angry red stained fifteen-year-old Rajula's delicately etched face. She threw off the blanket, deliberately exposing her legs, slender and pale as the trunk of a banana tree. Her *jhaguli*, the ankle-length garment young girls commonly wore in her village, had ridden up. Her mother's finely cut lips tightened. 'Get dressed immediately, Rajula,' she said. 'Can't you hear the goat bells tinkling? People are beginning to leave.'

Rajula sighed and jumped out of bed. Immediately, Ija began to roll up her bedding.

As she splashed chilly water over her face, Rajula's thoughts veered between the captivating memories of her dream and the journey that lay ahead. Despite the irritation she had displayed, the prospect of a trip to the lowlands excited her. And her mother knew it. Wasn't Rajula always asking about distant lands and the people who lived in them? She longed to accompany her father on his trading trips to far-off places, but being a girl, she would never be allowed.

'Those areas are unhealthy,' her mother would say, 'rife with disease. The weather is always bad and the air unclean. Why do you want to go there?'

'But Ija, I want to see for myself! The landscape, the people—they're very different from us, you said.'

'How would it help you?' Ganguli would reply. 'Soon you will get married and leave for Tibet. That is a different land, too.'

'Ah . . . but Tibet, where the Huniyas live, is too far over the mountains.' Rajula pouted. 'I wish Baujyu had promised me in marriage somewhere else. Somewhere in the lowlands.'

'Hush! Don't say that again. Your father will be furious. He has betrothed you to a powerful and wealthy man. You will live like a queen.'

Rajula's eyes narrowed as she examined her mother closely. She often wondered why there was never any conviction in Ija's voice when she said that—almost as if she were forcing herself to echo Baujyu's words. But she also knew that though as his only child, Baujyu indulged her more than other fathers did, he was set on this marriage and nothing would make him change his mind.

A long line of sheep, goats, mules and ponies snaked down the rough mountain track. Men dressed in homespun woollen coats and tight-fitting trousers, and women in wide black *ghaghras*, with *kaamalas* or large shawls wrapped around their bodies, and brocade-edged scarves tied on their heads, accompanied them. Big, shaggy-haired dogs loped alongside, while musicians crooned songs, thumping on small drums. Though the sun was bright, the air had a knifing edge. It was mid-January, the severest part of winter, and snow covered even the lowest reaches of the Himalayas.

Tramping along mechanically amid a gaggle of giggling girls, Rajula welcomed the chill slapping her cheeks. It would help to clear her head. The dream still had her in its thrall and in dazzling daylight it was somewhat disorienting. Once more, she ran over the sequence of events, so clear, unlike most dreams that faded the moment you woke up.

She had been sitting by a river, her feet dangling in the cool water. Suddenly a young man's face had printed itself on the ripples. Astonished, she had turned and found a pair of honey-brown eyes gazing into hers. The man had held out a hand, and puppet-like, she had offered hers. He had just been about to speak when her mother's voice had intruded and the dream had dissolved.

This dream had been haunting her night after night, for several weeks. Frustratingly, each time she had woken up before he could say anything. She shivered, recalling the tales old women narrated as they huddled around the fire at night—of demons that possessed young girls and drove them crazy. But how could he be a demon? His face was so gentle.

Rajula sighed. If only the day would pass soon so she could return to this mysterious world again! But . . . she should banish such thoughts. She was to marry Rikhyepal. Acid tears seared her eyelids. From far behind, she heard her father's voice ring out, authoritative as ever. Almost as if he were warning her not to stray from the path he had mapped out for her.

Sunapati Shauka, the wealthiest amongst the Shauka traders. He stood tall amid his fellows. And while his laugh might be the loudest, his frown made people tremble. Few dared oppose him. She thought of the rumours—that he knew magic, had enslaved powerful spirits.

As a child she had run to her mother once, asking her if it was true. Her mother's lovely face had frozen. 'Don't ever repeat those words. People say that because they envy your father.'

Rajula had sensed an untruth in that reply, even though she was just eight at the time. And a couple of years later, she had found out for herself.

It was during one of the usual halts they made in the course of their journeys up and down the mountains, trading their goods. Rajula had taken the goats up to a meadow to graze. Sprawled on her stomach, lazily chewing a stem of the sweet-sour *khatmith* grass, her wandering eyes were arrested by a sudden movement. She sat up to catch a glimpse of her father. There was no mistaking his purposeful stride as he hurried into a cave that lay some distance below the pasture. Something about the way he paused at the entrance, threw a quick glance all around, as if to check if anyone was watching, aroused her curiosity. She rose, her heartbeat quickening. What was he doing in the cave? Did . . . did it have any connection with the stories she'd heard? She had to find out! But suppose he caught her? She could always make some excuse, say that she came there by chance.

Swiftly, she had sped down the narrow goat track, careful not to dislodge stones or make any other sound that might give her away. When she reached the cave, a low, monotonous hum came to her ears. It was her father's voice all right, repeating rhythmic words—like a mantra being chanted. Rajula halted, uncertain. Something about the tone—its insistent, hypnotic drone—made her skin crawl. She wanted to get away at once. But to come so far and not find out! Holding her breath, she crept closer, even dared to peep in.

The cave was dark. Her father seemed to be in a trance as the indistinct sounds poured from his mouth in a muted nasal monotone.

Then Rajula turned to stone. Wisps of vapour were creeping out of the leather satchel he always carried—and taking terrifying shape. As she watched, a wavering figure floated in the air, visible even in the inky darkness. When an unreal voice began to emerge, something like the harsh rustle of leaves scraping each other during a storm, she willed her legs to move, and ran. She'd seen enough.

2

A Surprise Betrothal

Since that frightening day when Rajula had followed him to the cave, her beloved father had felt like a mysterious stranger—someone to avoid and fear.

When, just a few months ago he had returned from one of his trading trips to Tibet, or Hundesh as they called it, in high spirits, she had not attached any significance to it. He had probably earned a fine profit on the goods he had carried there. And when her mother told her that he had sent for her, she thought he simply wanted to show her the gifts he always brought back from these journeys.

She had noticed a peculiar tightness in the air though, a stiffness in her parents' expressions, too, as if they had quarrelled—which was rare. Her mother was compliant by nature and hardly ever opposed her father's strong will.

'Come, my child,' her father had stroked her head. An affectionate smile softened the harsh lines of his face. 'How I missed my little bird and her cheerful chirping on my long travels. Ah . . . what a pleasure it is to be back home again!'

'Was your trip very gruelling this time, Baujyu?' Rajula looked up at him, concerned. She had heard a lot about the arduous journey to Tibet, over snowy mountains, facing the threat of blizzards and avalanches, wolves and robbers. When she was younger, she would cling to him when he was about to leave and demand, 'Why do you go, Baujyu? Why do you risk your life?'

'Ah, child!' he would sigh. 'It is not in my destiny to lead an easy existence, enjoying the company of my wife and child. If I do not go, how will we earn money for your food, your clothes? Even this house we live in needed money to be built. The lowland people lead a comfortable life with their wide fields that produce so much grain. To travel constantly is our fate.' He had paused and added, 'Just as well that it is also in our blood. We do not know or care for any other kind of life.'

Rajula was well aware of that. As a people they liked to be always on the move. They needed to be as well, because of the harshness of the terrain, the unforgiving climate. They had to constantly search for better pastures for their sheep and goats, and travel throughout the year to trade their goods.

Now, her father produced a small silk pouch and took out a pair of earrings. Large oval turquoises set in gold. 'How do you like these?' he smiled.

Rajula's eyes widened. He had never brought back such a costly-looking gift, ever. For her mother maybe, but not for her. She felt a little frightened at the unexpectedness of it all, delighted as well, however, pleased at the importance it gave her. As if she were a grown-up, not a little girl any longer. 'Oh, Baujyu, they are beautiful! But weren't they very expensive?'

'Money is no object when it comes to my daughter. You are my only child, after all! All I have belongs to you.' Sunapati Shauka's eyes shone as he waved a dismissive hand in the air.

Her mother made a small movement and as Rajula turned to glance at her, she noticed that her eyes were moist. Rajula was well aware that her parents doted on her, because she was born late in their lives, after they had given up hope of having any children. And that her mother had conceived only after a visit to the temple of Chitrashila Devi, the patron of childless women. But as she watched, her mother's delicate eyebrows began to bunch in a dissatisfied frown. Rajula was startled to glimpse the angry glance she darted at her father.

He ignored it, turned and produced a larger pouch from his bag, a rather ornate one made of red-and-gold silk brocade. Rajula felt a little thrill of excitement. Once her father had brought some of this precious fabric for her mother, to make into a blouse. She knew it came from China and was high-priced. Was this a gift for her mother?

She couldn't help feeling a little proud that her father was rich enough to afford such extravagant gifts.

Sunapati Shauka's smile stretched from ear to ear now. Rajula could not understand why it made her uneasy, rather than happy, to see him in such a good mood. Probably because her mother was not smiling at all. Puzzled, her eyes shuttled between their faces. What was wrong?

'Look at this!' her father proclaimed, pulling something out of the pouch. Rajula started, as if one of his vaporous spirits would emerge. Instead, she saw a heavy gold necklace, studded with multicoloured stones.

'Ija!' she cried, clutching her mother's arm. 'Isn't it gorgeous?'

Ija stiffened and did not make any other response. Rajula's heartbeat fluttered like a disoriented butterfly. She noticed the warning glance that sparked swiftly from her father's eyes to her mother's, before the smile replaced it again.

'My dear, it is for you!'

'For me? Such an expensive necklace?' Rajula's head swam.

Sunapati Shauka cleared his throat. 'It . . . it is a special gift.' He looked at her fondly. 'I have wonderful news for you. Word of your beauty has spread far and wide, my girl.' Rajula flushed. She was always embarrassed when anyone mentioned her good looks. 'It has even crossed the high mountains to reach Tibet . . . and . . . a mighty ruler,

Rikhyepal, sent a proposal through an emissary, while I had halted at an inn in their territory. He expressed the desire to marry you.' Rajula felt even dizzier. Was she hearing right? 'And . . . I agreed, naturally. You will be a queen, my child, you will live in a palace.' His voice went up in excitement and he gave her a rare hug. 'This is just one of the gifts he sent.'

'Oh . . .' All colour fled from Rajula's face and strength seemed to drain away from her body, too. If her mother had not caught her, she might have fallen.

'Sit! Sit down, child! I know this is too sudden for you,' her father said anxiously. He paused. 'Rajula . . . we love you dearly and would never want to be parted from you. But it is the duty of parents to settle their children in life. And few girls will be settled as well as you, my little bird. Very few. I wish you all happiness.' His hands felt heavy on Rajula's head as he patted her in blessing.

'Raju, child . . .' Ija spoke for the first time. Her words rushed out, almost blurring with urgency. 'I know this has come as a shock. But the time comes when a girl has to get married and . . . her parents try to find the best match they can . . . .' She brushed away the tears that were spilling from her eyes. 'Your . . . your father has done his best.' Her voice choked up. 'I wish you all happiness, my child.'

Somehow, Rajula pulled herself together to fold her hands and bow to her father. 'I . . . I thank you, respected Baujyu, for arranging such a good marriage from me.' Her voice quavered as she said this, but she was relieved to see the frown that was puckering her father's brow disappear and a broad smile curl his lips again.

'Heaven grant that you always be happy, child! Ganguli, show Rajula the other gifts, the brocade gowns, the gold embroidered slippers and the other jewels her fiancé has sent. Oh, and the dried and candied fruits, too. All this is just a token. Just wait for the wedding–then you will see what a brilliant match I've made for you. Better still, our whole community will gain. He has promised special benefits to us as traders.'

Rajula had gazed at the array of gifts, befuddled. Her fiancé! Like every other girl her age in the village, she knew she would get married sooner or later. The murmurs that she had reached the right age for marriage and that a suitable groom should be found for her had been buzzing in her ears for quite some time. Two of her friends had got married that summer; another was betrothed and would wed in winter. But to go away and live in Tibet! She could hardly have imagined that her father would consider such a thing.

Rajula's feet were unsteady as she accompanied her mother back to her own room.

'Ija, why didn't you tell me?' she cried, the moment her father was out of earshot.

'I wanted to let your father give the news himself.' Her mother's voice was expressionless.

'You . . . you don't like this match, do you?' The words flew out of Rajula's mouth.

'Hush!' Her mother put a hand on Rajula's mouth and looked around fearfully. 'Your father did his best,' she repeated. Her voice dropped, 'I . . . I did have other hopes . . . But what good would it have done had I protested?'

'What hopes, Ija?' Rajula whispered into her mother's breast.

'Nothing, nothing. It's a woman's lot to endure.' She sighed. 'Hundesh is so far away. Who knows when you'll be able to visit us, once you get married! But . . . I hope you'll always be happy, my child.' She hugged Rajula so tightly that she squeezed the breath out of her.

A gathering chill was beginning to numb Rajula's limbs. Her friends had been so excited at the thought of getting married, entering the world of adults. Why did her heart plummet, why did she feel so apprehensive? Her mother's words added to her fears. Why was it a woman's lot to always bear whatever the men decided for them? But as memories of what she had witnessed in the cave so long ago surfaced, she knew she could not dare to protest.

The dreams had begun that very night, creating further turmoil. What did they mean? Who was this young man? And why did she long to escape into the dream to be with him? Was . . . was her father using his magic to test her? The thought was insane. But her life had changed so unexpectedly that anything seemed possible now.

3

The Fair

A languorous peace overcame Rajula as her gaze wandered in the depths of the valleys that criss-crossed before her. Light and shade, sharp purple mountain edges brushed with gold by the winter sun, streams like crumpled strips of silver streaking past black clumps of rock. Closer to her, dark green deodar trees stood firm and tall, while oaks turned the silvery undersides of their leaves against the breeze. A variety of shrubs spotted the hillside—rhododendron, juniper and goat's-thorn—though the January frost had wilted the grass. Large, glossy black crows hopped about, their squawking punctuated by a woodpecker's insistent *tok-tok-tok* from a nearby tree. They had stopped to enjoy a snack and a brief rest before they tramped on to their destination, Bageshwar. She had never felt so relaxed since the day her father had broken the news of her engagement to her.

Her friend Bhaguli spoilt it all. 'This might be the last time you attend the Uttarayani Fair, Raju,' she teased. Her coal-black eyes glittered as she squeezed Rajula's arm with short, plump fingers.

'Might be yours, too!' Rajula retorted sharply. Bhaguli was to be married next month.

'Why mine?' Bhaguli pouted. 'I can continue to come each year.'

'Only if your husband wants to bring you,' Rajula's reply was swift. 'My mother doesn't get to go each time.'

'Oh, stop it, you two!' Their third friend Saru cried out. 'Who knows what will happen when? But Raju, how will you manage to live in Tibet? Their ways will be so different!'

Bhaguli burst out laughing. 'How will you talk to your husband? You'll have to use sign language. Suppose he gets annoyed when you can't understand what he says? *Oh babba!*'

'Hunh . . . it'll be his job to understand me!' Rajula snapped. 'He was the one eager to marry me—not I!'

The two friends were struck dumb for a moment. Finally, Saru spoke, 'She's right, Bhaga. Everyone says he sought our Raju because she's like a heavenly *apsara* come to earth. But Raju, you never showed us the fabulous gifts people say he sent.'

Rajula pulled a face. 'You can come and see them any time you want,' she shrugged.

'What a girl!' Bhaguli exclaimed. 'Anyone else would have been eager to show off the gold and the silks they say you received. But of course, a Tibetan king would send double of what an ordinary—oh—stop it! Stop!'

She writhed with laughter as Rajula began to pinch and tickle her.

'You stop going on about my future husband,' Rajula giggled.

'Get up, girls, it's time to move on!' It was Rajula's mother. She threw them a sharp glance. 'What's so funny?'

Her tone was brusque, but Rajula sensed that she was happy to see her laughing in such a carefree manner, after a long, long time.

The sun had slid a good way towards the horizon when they stretched out their tents on a level piece of ground high above the valley. The girls did what they could, driving the sheep and goats that had accompanied them into the pen that was quickly set up. The dogs helped them, of course, skilfully herding the animals. Soon the cooking fires were licking round the pots and the sharp aroma of red chillies and garlic sizzling in hot mustard oil began to stoke their hunger. The march always stirred up their appetites. Men squatted on the ground in little groups, munching nuts, punctuating the anecdotes they were exchanging with loud cracks as they broke walnuts open.

Rajula drew a deep breath. It was always thrilling to set up camp in a new place, but this town, Bageshwar was special. They visited once a year at the time of the Uttarayani Fair in mid-January, when they would find plenty of customers for their goods. Uttarayani was an important festival. It was the day the sun entered the Makar zodiacal sign and began to move north. They also called it Ghughuti and celebrated by feeding crows sweets made of flour and jaggery in the shape of the small dove called *ghughuti*. People gathered in hordes to take a purifying bath at the confluence of the rivers Saryu and Gomti at Bageshwar. Crowded, bustling with energy—what a contrast this place was to the quiet meadows she was used to!

From the camp, the valley looked as if it had been carelessly splashed with brilliant colour. Snatches of song came to Rajula's ear and fascinating scents wafted up. A strange sadness gripped her. Bhaguli was right. Once she got married, she might never experience this again. How would she cross the high mountains? And why would her husband let her come? Then she determinedly brushed away the rebellious tears that pricked her eyelids. Why worry about the future? She should concentrate on enjoying the present as much as she could.

She slipped into a sound sleep, soon after dinner was done. When she awoke the next morning, she got the vague feeling that something was different—and not just the new surroundings. Realization slammed her with stunning force. The dream had not visited her last night!

She sat there dazed, conscious of a peculiar emptiness. The dream was disturbing. All the same, it had become such an essential part of her life. Why had it vanished? A weary gloom overtook her, a hollow feeling of betrayal. After winning her heart, had the man of her dreams abandoned her? Or was the change in scene responsible for it? Was he a spirit who resided in a particular place? Or . . . her father's magic? The last thought made her shudder.

As she crouched there, head clutched in her hands, she heard her mother call. 'Rajula! Come, child, we're all going to the river to bathe. We'll pay our respects to Lord Baghnath after that.'

Rajula experienced a spasm of irritation. She wanted to be left alone to think, to puzzle over this peculiar happening. 'Ija, the water will be so cold!' The protest was almost automatic.

'You silly girl! How can you not take a dip in the river? Why did we come here, if not to bathe there at this auspicious time?'

Reluctantly Rajula rose. Maybe it would come back. Dreams were like that.

Another thought cheered her up even more. Maybe she could appeal to Lord Baghnath for help and guidance. She hurriedly gathered up a set of clothes, and joined her friends and the other women hurrying towards the river.

The crowds of people thronging the banks made her nervous—so many that the town seemed to be flowing into the river. People shopping, taking ritual dips, chanting prayers, or eating. A jumble of sound assailed her ears—the lowing of cows, the shrill music of a festive pipe, the drone of a priest's voice, children laughing and yelling—was there anything missing from the scene?

Shivering, giggling, Rajula dunked herself in the cold water, along with her friends. Then they chased each other out and hurriedly changed into dry clothes.

'What are you going to ask for, Raju?' Bhaguli whispered. 'I'm going to ask for a happy married life and prosperity for my future husband. But . . . yours is already so prosperous.'

Rajula bit down her irritation. This constant harping on her husband's wealth infuriated her. To her, this betrothal was like some fantasy her father had conjured up. Her dream was far more real.

Suddenly she knew what she would pray for. That she be united with the man of her dreams. Yes, that's what she would ask for, most fervently. Perhaps Lord Baghnath would answer her prayers.

Sure enough, as she stood before the god of tigers, she closed her eyes and begged, 'Please, Lord Baghnath, please grant my wish. They say you are powerful beyond all belief, that you answer any prayer that comes from the heart. Grant me a husband who will love me and whom I love. Let him be the man of my dreams!'

She reached up to ring the bell again as they left the temple, stroked the two tiger images that guarded it. As they tramped back to the camp, she kept up with Bhaguli and Saru's chatter mechanically. Fortunately they were so intrigued by the incessant bustle around them that they did not notice her preoccupation.

Rajula gazed at it all as if from a distance. Women decked up in red-spotted yellow veils, their *ghaghras* flaring like huge, gaudy umbrellas, enormous gold nose rings that almost hid their faces and the vermilion marks stretching up their noses through the partings in their hair. Men had flowers tucked in their caps, and their gold earrings glinted merrily as they moved. She had never seen so many different kinds of people gathered in one place, yet, she felt strangely disinterested in everything.

Back in their camp, there was the murmur of strange voices. Men were beginning to straggle in, seeking the goods her father had brought from Tibet.

After a hurried breakfast Sunapati Shauka began to display them—borax, rock salt and asafoetida, skeins of the yarn they had been spinning from raw clumps of wool ever since he returned, some of the rugs and woollen cloth her mother had been weaving through the year. And on special request, precious gold dust.

Then she heard her friends calling out, 'Rajula!

Aren't you coming? We're taking the goats to graze on the hillside!'

Her father glanced up from the midst of his bargaining. 'You stay here!' His eyes were stern, banishing the euphoria that had begun to grip her.

'Oh, please let me go, Baujyu!' Rajula didn't know how these audacious words burst out. 'There is still some good grass here, we'll get better milk!'

Sunapati frowned at her for a moment, then seemed to relent. 'All right,' he shrugged. 'But be sure to return long before dark.'

'Of course we will!' All three girls chorused. They scampered away, as light on their feet as the goats. In this sheltered valley, the sun's rays felt so pleasantly warm on their backs, that it instantly raised their spirits.

They had gone quite a distance—the camp was no longer visible—when the sight of a sparkling rivulet made Rajula pause. It looked puzzlingly familiar. A small temple stood close by, nestling in a narrow ledge higher up the incline.

'Come on!' cried her friends. 'Let's go a little higher up.'

'I want to visit the temple for a minute,' she replied. 'I'll catch up with you. Just . . . just keep an eye on my goats.'

'Since when have you become so religious? You've already paid your respects to Lord Baghnath,' Bhaguli asked.

'Leave her alone,' Saru nudged her as she caught the expression on Rajula's face. 'Don't take long, Raju,' she added in a gentler tone.

4

An Unexpected Encounter

Rajula watched her friends scrambling up the slope. The grass was splayed out in dry brown wisps, but leafy bushes and herbs added a touch of green. The goats would get plenty to eat. But what impulse had impelled her to halt here? Almost as if someone had planted the thought in her head? She glanced up at the temple, then at the stream again. An unbearable longing came over her—to dip her feet in the water. How crazy! She had protested when her mother asked her to come and bathe in the river. She should run to the temple, say her prayers and rejoin her friends.

But the stream . . . it beckoned her . . . and why did it look so familiar? She must have seen it during her earlier visits—though she didn't have a strong memory of the temple. She was visiting Bageshwar after a gap of several years. Surrendering to the mysterious urge, she turned impatiently.

She stood near the brook for a while, gazing at her reflection. Then she knelt and perched on a rock, hesitantly dipped her feet into a little pool. The water was chillier than the river but not unpleasant. As she watched the little ripples radiating out and stroked the smooth pebbles with her feet, her skin prickled. She knew why it was so familiar . . . she had been seeing this rivulet in her dreams . . . night after night.

A peculiar dread was beginning to clutch at her, quickening her breath, when the sound of a horse's hooves made her start. Rajula froze. Who could it be? She was all alone in this lonely spot. She had been very foolish—to have parted company with her friends.

She did not dare to turn and find out, hoping the person would pass on. The minutes stretched out unbearably, as she sat there petrified. But the horse seemed to have halted. Then she heard footsteps advancing towards her, behind her back. As they came closer, some instinct forced her to act. She began to inch her feet out of the water, then pulled them up with a cry. What was that in the water? The reflection of a face, right next to hers! A young man's face. A face she knew . . .

She heard him gasp, 'Are you real? Or has a goddess taken human shape?'

For a moment Rajula could not summon up the courage to either reply or turn to look at him. She just could not tear her eyes away from the image in the water . . . Was it really the face of the man who had been haunting her dreams—night after night after night?

'Won't you speak? Or are you angry that I've disturbed you? I beg your forgiveness. I . . . I'll go away, if you want.' His voice was as gentle as the murmur of the wind in the pines. Who was he? The way he spoke showed that he was certainly not from around the area where she lived.

Rajula could almost catch the steady rhythm of his heartbeat as he waited for her to respond. Then there was a long-drawn-out sigh and the wisp of a sound as if someone was turning away.

She whirled. 'I . . . I'm no goddess, just an ordinary girl,' she stammered. Her heart was bursting out of her ribs. 'But . . . are *you* real?'

'As real as you! But why do you say that?'

Overwhelmed, she barely registered that he was much taller than any man she had met, and his muscular shoulders seemed to strain at the fabric of his fine woollen *angarakha*. As her eyes skimmed over his frame she got the impression of wealth, far beyond any she had ever encountered.

Rajula screwed her eyes shut. Was she imagining it all? She had to make sure. Hesitantly, she opened her eyes and examined his face again, long and hard.

Just then his mouth crinkled into a playful smile as he said, 'Lovely maiden, could you please give me some water to drink?'

Befuddled, Rajula cupped her hands and scooped up some water from the stream. Before she could rise, the man slid to the ground in one lithe movement, kneeling beside her. And just as she was about to pour the water into his hands, he caught hold of hers. Startled, Rajula was about to jerk away when he began to drink from her hands. She sprang up.

'What are you doing? Is . . . is this the way to behave with a girl?'

The man laughed apologetically, then shook his head. 'Forgive me. It is wrong to take such liberties, but I couldn't resist it. You are so enchanting.'

Rajula stared at him. 'Who *are* you?' she whispered.

'I'm Malushahi, the ruler of Katyur.'

The king of Katyur! Rajula almost keeled over. 'You can't be!' she exclaimed.

'Why not?'

Rajula's eyes dropped, her face turned red. How could she tell him? How could she ask him why he had he been visiting her in her dreams? There had to be some explanation.

'Why can't I be?' he repeated. There was an angry edge to his voice that provoked Rajula.

'Because—you look just like the man . . . who . . . has been appearing in my dreams . . .'

Malushahi gaped at her as if she were talking nonsense.

'It's true!' Rajula cried out. 'Why would I make up something like that? When I reached this place, this stream—it all looked so familiar. And when I saw you—I thought I had taken leave of my senses . . .' Her voice trailed away.

The large emerald in his ring glinted as he tugged at a stray lock of hair. 'This is the strangest thing I've heard. Who are you?'

'I . . . I'm Rajula . . . the daughter of Sunapati Shauka . . . from Jalnar Desh . . . and I'm already betrothed to the ruler of Hundesh,' she blurted out.

'Betrothed? If you have been seeing me in your dreams, it shows that you're meant for me. How can you marry anyone else?'

'I must go now,' Rajula took a quick step forward. What audacity! But . . . was it her own fault that this happened? After all, she had prayed to Lord Baghnath that she be united with the man of her dreams. How foolish she'd been! She could not have imagined that her prayers would be answered so promptly. Now it felt shamefully wrong. Her father had already given his word. Tears suddenly singed her eyes.

'Wait! What's the hurry?' he frowned. 'I'm not going to harm you.'

'My friends are waiting for me,' she said desperately. 'I had told them I wanted to pray at the temple. They must be getting worried. And . . . my father has promised me in marriage. I mustn't talk to strange men.'

'No! You can't just run away after telling me that you've been seeing me in your dreams. Don't you realize, Rajula? We were meant to meet. It was destined that you should be sitting here and I should pass this way.' The vehemence in his voice frightened her.

'But—I'm already betrothed.' Rajula covered her face with her hands.

'No, I cannot let you go. Listen to me, at least.' He drew a deep breath. 'The moment I set eyes on you, I was enchanted, Rajula! You well know . . . there are higher powers that decide our fates, rather than the wishes of men. All the signs show you were meant for me. And remember, I will keep you in luxury. You will dress in silk and velvet, wear the most precious jewels, feast on the finest rice, the sweetest of fruit, fresh fish from the river . . . What will you get in that desolate place?'

Rajula's head was awhirl as she took a hesitant step away from him. If she left now, she might never see him again. She had begged Lord Baghnath to let her meet him. The god might never answer another prayer if she spurned the king now. She should spend some time with him, at least . . . . But what if her father found out?

How would he? He was busy with his customers, confident that she was tending the goats with her friends. She turned and Malushahi's face lit up immediately. He reached out to her.

She didn't know how the blissful moments passed till the tinkle of goat bells brought her to her senses. 'My friends!' She started up. 'I must go!'

'Can't you wait a little longer?' he pleaded.

'No . . . as it is, I'll be besieged with questions.'

'Tomorrow then? I'll be here in the afternoon,' Malushahi whispered, drawing her close. 'You have to come.'

Rajula rushed into the temple and fell to her knees before the goddess. She stayed that way till she heard her friends calling to her.

'What happened to you?' Bhaguli asked, when she hurried out. 'We waited and waited, then decided you might want to be by yourself.'

'Are you all right?' Saru's round face was creased with concern.

'I . . . I'm all right,' Rajula nodded. 'I . . . went and sat by the river for a while.'

'What is this?' Bhaguli's sharp eyes had picked out a jewelled tassel that gleamed in the dried grass. 'And . . . see, the marks of horse's hooves. Did someone pass this way? I hope no one troubled you . . .'

Rajula's face grew hot. 'No! No! No one troubled me.'

Saru's eyes probed her so intensely that Rajula grew frightened. 'Let . . . let's go,' she said. 'Baujyu will get angry.'

'But what shall we do with this?' Bhaguli cried out. 'It looks very valuable. Who could it belong to?'

'Only a king could afford something like that,' Saru said thoughtfully.

'Rajula, did your fiancé come here to meet you?' Bhaguli's eyes sparkled with mischief. 'Perhaps he could not wait till the wedding.'

'Don't be silly!' Rajula's flush deepened. 'How could he come all the way from Hundesh?'

'The Huniyas know all kinds of magic, my mother says,' Bhaguli went on. 'It would be easy for him to fly over the mountains.'

'Stop it! Someone must have been riding this way and dropped it,' Saru said. 'Perhaps Malushahi, the king of Katyur, passed by. They say he is visiting the fair.'

Rajula stopped breathing. She darted ahead, in case they noticed that she was blushing. She was hugely relieved when the girls continued to chatter on mindlessly.

'*Babba-ho*, Malushahi? They say he is as handsome as a god. I would certainly like to set eyes on him. Did you see him by chance, Rajula? Is that why you remained stuck here? I would lose my senses, too . . .'

'Will you stop it?' Rajula whirled around in a fury. Bhaguli's banter frightened her. If word went around and reached her father, who knew the consequences? 'I'm sorry I stayed on here, but I've made a special vow to the goddess. Tomorrow I'll come again and pray. If you say all these silly things, my father will get suspicious and might not let me leave the camp.'

Bhaguli was instantly contrite. 'Forgive me, Raju,' she said, putting an arm around her shoulder. 'You know how my tongue runs away with me.'

'What shall we do with the tassel?' Saru asked.

With an effort Rajula concealed her longing. How she yearned to hold it in her hand! But she dared not show any interest. 'You could just keep it,' she said carelessly.

'No!' Bhaguli shook her head vehemently. 'My mother would ask all sorts of questions.'

'Why don't we just put it in the hollow in that tree trunk?' Saru said. 'It doesn't feel right to leave something so precious lying on the ground.'

'You are really clever,' Rajula gazed at Saru admiringly. Maybe . . . she could take it out later.

5
Catastrophe!

How could a dream turn into reality? Rajula shivered at the thought as she lay down to sleep. She had not really believed it could, even when she stood before the image of Lord Baghnath, praying with all her heart. How uncanny that it should stop, just the night before she met Malushahi. He was right. There were unknowable forces that ruled our destiny. But what would happen now? Her father had planned to get her married this summer. She shivered again, anticipating his wrath if things did not turn out the way he wanted.

Finally, she decided to banish all thought and resign herself to the machinations of whatever power was planning her future.

Her mother had decided to bathe in the holy river every day of their stay. So once again there was the ritual bath in the river, followed by prayers at the temple of Lord Baghnath. She thanked the god for answering her prayer and now begged him to sort out the confusion in her mind.

The fair began in earnest today—they had arrived a day earlier to settle in properly. Her friends were eager to savour its sights. Truly, it far surpassed their village markets in scale. Almost everything you could buy was on sale here, from food items to woollen rugs to brass and copper vessels to horses, cows, sheep or goats. Goods were laid out in baskets or piled in heaps on the ground. The girls strolled past, admiring, exclaiming, sometimes stooping to examine something. The pot-pourri of smells was overpowering, too. The coarse earthy smell of animal dung rose up in waves to battle the perfume of tobacco from hundreds of gurgling hookahs. Added to it was the appetizing aroma of puris being fried to be savoured with *alu gutak*, the spicy potato dish she loved. But nothing held Rajula's attention for long.

Her mother began to pick up the things that she would not be able to find back home. 'I need to prepare for your wedding, too,' she murmured.

Rajula's heart plummeted. If only she could tell her! But she knew it was no use, even if she did. Would Ija dare to oppose her father? Again, she pushed her anxieties aside, buoyed up by the thought of meeting Malushahi. How she longed for the minutes to hurry past! To get away from the constant buzz of the fair, rush to the quiet slopes with her beloved king. Even the foot-tapping beat of the drums that her friends were swaying to, failed to enthuse her, nor did the haunting lilt of voices raised in lively song as people linked arms in the *jhoda*, a popular folk dance.

As the afternoon sun began its downward march across the dome of the sky, Rajula's heartbeat quickened to an unbearable pace.

'Ija,' she whispered, 'I vowed to the goddess Angiyari Devi that I would pay my respects to her every day while I'm here.'

Her mother gazed at her for a while, then said, 'Come back soon. And . . . take your friends with you.'

Rajula glanced at them, enthralled with the spectacle of the dance, urging each other to join in. 'I don't think they want to leave,' she said.

Her mother nodded. 'All right,' she said reluctantly. 'Come back soon.'

Rajula hurried away. Her heart pounded like a crazy hammer as she sped over the slopes to the small temple.

Would he come? Was it foolish for her to believe that a king would keep his promise to an ordinary village girl like her?

When she caught sight of his imposing figure seated in the courtyard of the temple, she almost fainted.

Malushahi started when he saw her. 'What took you so long?'

'I couldn't get away!' Rajula cried. She rushed into the temple and bowed before the goddess. Malushahi followed her in.

'I can marry you right here,' he whispered.

'No!'

'You . . . you're refusing me?' Malushahi's eyes darkened with shock.

'No . . . I meant that I wouldn't like to get married like that . . . in secret. I . . . I want to marry you properly.'

'You are right.' Malushahi suddenly looked shamefaced. 'We will not be like Shakuntala and Dushyant. We'll take the seven steps in the presence of our loved ones. I'll go back to my capital city Bairath and tell my mother. She will have to convince your father that I'm a better match than the Tibetan. In the meantime . . . take a look at what I've brought for you!' He produced a pot of creamy yoghurt and a small basket containing sweets. 'Just taste them,' he said. 'You will not get anything like this in Hundesh.'

Rajula smiled. 'You never said all this in my dreams,' she said.

'You didn't give me a chance,' he laughed.

They strolled into a patch of pine forest close by and sat on a large flat rock. As Malushahi whispered into her ears and put his arms around her, Rajula felt that she had re-entered her enchanting dream. She wished it would never end.

The next afternoon, too, she went off by herself, using her vow to the goddess as an excuse, and the next afternoon and the next.

As the days passed, it became harder and harder for Malushahi and Rajula to part.

Malushahi would say, 'Just a few moments more, my Rajula. Do you know how hard it is to pass the hours away from you? I lie awake all night and the sweetest music cannot soothe my tortured soul. Why don't you just come with me to Bairath?'

'If only it were that easy,' Rajula would say. 'If only I had met you before my father promised me to the Tibetan ruler. But there's one thing I cannot understand. I began to dream about you only from the day my father informed me about the betrothal. And the dreams stopped the night before I met you in person . . . Why?'

'It means that the gods do not want you to marry the Tibetan.'

'It . . . it feels the same way to me, too,' Rajula sighed. Her voice dropped to a whisper, 'But I fear my father's wrath . . . and his magic powers. I . . . I fear he'll do you terrible harm once he finds out.'

'I do not fear your father,' Malushahi said. 'My guru has great powers, too. He will protect me.'

'Sh-ssh! Don't say such things,' Rajula looked around uneasily.

A strange premonition had hung over her since the morning. Matters had been proceeding too smoothly. She peered through the tall pine trees that surrounded them. A shred of mist seemed to be draped over the branches of the one closest to them—something unusual on a clear day. It reminded her uncomfortably of what she had witnessed in the cave, years and years ago—the vapour emerging from her father's satchel. 'It's getting really late, my Malu,' she said with a shiver. 'How soon darkness falls in this season. I'm afraid to go home all alone.'

'I've told you I can escort you back, following you at a distance on my horse.'

'No, no! People might notice. Let me go now . . .' She clung to him for a few moments, then tore herself away.

Rajula ran all the way, but it was already dusk when she reached the camp.

Sunapati Shauka was pacing up and down like an enraged panther.

'Where did you go, you shameless girl?' he roared. 'Don't give me the lie about going to the temple. You think your father is a fool? Have you forgotten that you are already betrothed?' His next words made Rajula's head reel. 'And . . . are you stupid enough to believe Malushahi will marry you? We are self-respecting people; I did not raise you to be the plaything of kings! Get inside!'

Trembling, Rajula sank to the floor of the tent. How had her father discovered that she had been meeting Malushahi? Her friends could not have told on her. Since she needed their help, eventually she had confided in them and sworn them to secrecy. She recalled the wisp of vapour in the forest and shuddered.

Her mother burst in. She crouched next to her and held her close. 'What have you done, you foolish child,' she whispered. 'Why didn't you tell me? I would have found a way to help you.'

Rajula stared at her. The resolution in Ija's voice astounded her. She was about to speak, when her mother put a warning finger on her lips. She heard the familiar brisk, firm tread of her father's feet outside.

'I'll bring you something to eat,' Ija said. Then her voice sank to a whisper. 'Better to keep out of his way tonight.'

Ija rose and slipped out of the tent. It felt like an age when she finally returned with a brass *thali* filled with food.

Somehow, Rajula swallowed a few morsels of the rotis and *saag* her mother had brought her. Her tears just wouldn't stop. What would happen now? She should have listened to Malushahi and married him in the temple. Or not allowed herself to give in to the temptation of meeting him over and over again. But how could she have resisted it? The only blessing was perhaps that her father had not returned to harangue her again. She sat there, listening for his footsteps, dreading the moment he would enter the tent.

Finally, utterly worn out, she rolled herself in her blanket and lay down.

'Get up, Rajula, hurry!' It was her mother's voice.

'Wh-what? What's the matter, Ija? It's still so dark!'

'Hurry, your father wants to leave right away. There's no time for questions.'

'Rajula! Is the girl up, Ganguli?' Sunapati Shauka's voice sliced through the thick of the night.

Somehow, Rajula got to her feet. Her legs felt as weak as water, but she had to rouse herself. What did her father want now?

She soon found out. The discovery came as a blow so shattering that she almost collapsed to the ground again.

He had decided to leave Bageshwar right away without waiting for dawn to break. The tents were already being dismantled, the animals loaded. Rajula tottered out, shivering.

'Get on your pony!' Her father's voice, harsher than she had ever heard it, made her jump. Somehow she climbed on. Some of the pack animals were beginning to move already. The tinkling of their bells, normally so cheerful, had an ominous sound today. The sheep baaed agitatedly, confused at this change in their routine, and the goats added their own tremulous clamour.

Sunapati Shauka shook the reins of Rajula's horse and clicked his tongue. 'Get moving,' he said.

Rajula clutched the reins as the pony leapt forward. Her heart felt like a lump of lead. How could it all end like this? As unexpectedly as it had begun. Were the gods toying with her? Why had Baghnath granted her wish, only to snatch it away? Tears overflowed her eyes, traced a scorching path down her frozen cheeks.

The thought throbbed inside her painfully—what would Malushahi think when she did not turn up the next day? Would he believe she was fickle? If only she could send him a message! But there was no time, and no one she could trust close by. Then a terrifying thought numbed her heart.

Would her father hurry the wedding and send her to Tibet right away?

6

Heartbreak

The return home was as dismal as the journey out had been fun-filled. Worse, when day broke, the sun had hidden itself, too, appearing only as a faint glimmer of light behind a pall of dark clouds. Soon, chilly needles of rain began to descend, accompanied by a freezing wind.

The village felt so silent when they arrived, like a hamlet peopled only by ghosts. The weather had driven everyone who had remained behind indoors and they were probably huddled around fires. In any case, except for a few old men and women, most of the people had gone to the fair. The thud of the horses' hooves and the baaing of the sheep aroused enough curiosity for a couple of doors to open and some shrill voices to call out, asking why they had returned and if all was well.

'There is nothing wrong. Just that my daughter is a little sick.' Sunapati Shauka's voice grew gruffer as he was compelled to repeat these words over and over again.

But how could the truth stay hidden? Whether one of her father's attendants let it out or the wind conveyed it mysteriously, soon, the real reason for their early return became common knowledge. Before long, old crones began to come and visit Ganguli, hunkered down on the floor, slurping tea from brass tumblers, their comments sharp with sting and venom. Some proclaimed, clicking their tongues, that beauty like Rajula's was a curse rather than a blessing. Others, that the sooner girls were married off, the better. Their malevolent words seared Rajula's ears as she crouched in a corner of her room, marvelling at her mother's patience in listening to all that talk without flaring up.

When the others returned from the fair, it became far worse. Her father's frown dug deeper into his forehead; his voice acquired a permanently rough edge. Rajula stayed out of his way, even though it was hard to in the narrow spaces in which they lived, and confined to the house as she was now.

He had laid down the law soon after they returned. 'If I see you or hear you have been anywhere outside these four walls, you brazen girl, I'll bury you in the snow with my own hands!' His upraised finger was so menacing as he growled out the words that Rajula had to press her hand tightly against her mouth to keep from crying out.

'I don't want to go anywhere,' she wanted to say. All she wanted was to see her beloved Malushahi, at least once again. She wanted to tell him that she loved him truly and always would, even if she married someone else. But how could she?

She was not even allowed to meet her friends. How shocked she was when her mother turned Bhaguli and Saru away, saying, 'I'm so sorry, but she's too unwell to meet anyone.'

'Oh, can't we see her for just a few minutes, to cheer her up?' Bhaguli began, when Sunapati Shauka stormed out.

'You dare to argue?' he yelled. 'Haven't you heard what Rajula's mother said? You cannot meet her! You girls have no respect for your elders!'

Bhaguli gasped. 'Sorry, please forgive me, Kaka,' she murmured tearfully.

Rajula stuffed her head cloth into her mouth to suppress her sobs. If her father overheard, he'd be furious.

'You did well, keeping those girls away,' he muttered to her mother. 'Remember now, never to let Rajula out of your sight.'

Ija's steps were slow and heavy as she entered the room. 'Hush,' she said, gathering her into her arms. 'Your father loves you. He doesn't want you to come to any harm, to be disrespected by anyone.'

'Are you sure?' Rajula wanted to ask. 'Isn't this the worst thing for me, not to ever be able to see Malu again?' But she had no choice but to keep silent. Despite her best efforts, however, a low cry burst out.

'Don't give up hope, child,' Ija whispered, squeezing her tight. 'Have faith in Baghnath.'

Rajula's heart almost stopped beating. She brushed away her tears and stared at her mother. Ija's expression was mysterious. A faint smile lit her face as she stroked Rajula's hair.

'How can you say this, Ija?' Rajula asked. 'You know that the moment the weather improves even slightly, Baujyu will fix the date for my marriage and . . . I'll have to go away to that cold, distant land. Forever.' She let out a shuddering sigh. 'I wonder if I'll ever see you again . . .'

'Don't say that, my child.' Ija clutched her closer. 'I told you, never give up hope.'

Rajula did not dare question her mother further, but she tried to follow her advice. The pale, freezing winter days dragged on and on. She clung to the memory of the wonderful moments she had spent with Malushahi, and refused to surrender to the dark gloom that was threatening to drag her down. She tried to keep herself occupied with household chores and fought to remain hopeful as she coaxed yarn from wool or sat on the loom, weaving cloth with her mother. Malushahi would surely find her, take her away . . . he was a powerful king.

Then the snow began to melt and fruit blossoms hesitantly sprouted on dry branches. Blossoms gave way to fruit, as spring turned into summer. As preparations began for the Shaukas' move to the higher altitudes, Rajula was gripped by a terrible restlessness. The weather had improved, and was not so hazardous any longer. Why hadn't Malushahi come? Or sent his mother as he'd promised? Had he forgotten her already? Were all his tender words just for effect? Or did he believe that she did not love him equally? If only she could find a way to reach him and prove her love was true! This thought gripped her all through the journey north, while jogging along on her pony, or camping in a flower strewn meadow when night fell. It did not leave her even when they reached their final destination, the small village beside the Goriganga river where they spent summer.

7
A Startling Discovery

Then one day, she overheard an extraordinary conversation between her parents, which made goose pimples rise like a rash on her skin.

'You are breaking your promise!' Her mother sounded almost frantic. 'Don't you fear the goddess's wrath?'

'You speak like a foolish woman, Ganguli!' Sunapati snapped. 'Do you actually believe that the king of Katyur would honour a promise made before he was born? Why didn't his mother seek us out, if she meant to be true to her word?'

'Malushahi is god-fearing—from what I have heard. His mother Dharma Devi, too, is deeply religious, we know. Who knows what might have prevented her from searching for us! And who else but Chitrashila Devi could be behind Rajula and Malushahi's chance meeting? Their overpowering love for each other? I beg you, do not invite her anger. There is still time to make amends.'

'I have given my word to Rikhyepal.' Sunapati's tone was hard and set. 'He, too, is a noble king. If Malushahi's mother meant to honour her promise, she would have sought us out long ago.'

Promise? What promise? Rajula's heart thumped madly, like an out-of-control drum. Why hadn't she been told about it? An icy chill trickled down her spine. Was this why her dreams about Malushahi had started to appear exactly on the day her father informed her about her engagement? If only she could tell her mother! Didn't it sound like divine intervention? But would her father pay any attention? He would probably dismiss it as a story she'd made up and become even more furious. All the same, she longed to ask her mother about the promise. When it was made and why? What had actually transpired at Chitrashila Devi's temple?

That night, she got her answers. As she lay beside her mother trying not to toss and turn, Ija whispered: 'My child, there's something I want to say . . . I . . . I feel guilty I never told you this earlier.'

'What . . . what is it, Ija?' Rajula burst out.

Her mother sighed again. 'What you feel for Malushahi . . . what he feels for you . . . I think it did not happen by chance. It . . . it's most likely ordained by Chitrashila Devi.'

'What-what do you mean, Ija?' Rajula's skin tightened around her.

'It has to be! She must have chosen this for you. And I'm so afraid that your father's stubbornness will bring calamity upon us.'

'What are you saying, Ija?'

'This . . . this happened . . . about ten months before you were born . . .' Ganguli paused and took hold of Rajula's hand. 'You know this, that for many years after our marriage, your father and I were not blessed with children. I prayed and fasted . . . we visited many holy men and temples, even tried all kinds of herbal remedies, but I still remained childless. Then someone advised us to go and pray at Chitrashila Devi's temple.'

'You've told me all this earlier, Ija.' Rajula tried not to be impatient.

'True, but listen to the rest. We encountered another couple on a similar mission there—a noble-looking man and a charming lady. We learned that they were Dulashahi and Dharma Devi, the king and queen of Katyur. For some reason, Dharma and I took an instant liking to each other . . . almost as if we had been sisters in a previous birth. She made me exchange a vow: 'If you have a daughter and I a son, promise me that we will get them married,' she insisted. Overwhelmed, I agreed at once. We applied a *tika* on each other's bellies, which symbolized our wombs, to emphasize the sacredness of this promise.'

'Is this true?' Rajula gasped.

'As true as I am lying here beside you. Well . . . ten

months after our visit, you arrived like a blessing, my child.' Ganguli stroked Rajula's head tenderly. 'And when some time later, we heard that Dulashahi and Dharma Devi had been blessed with a son, too, I felt I was walking on air. I brought you up with care, exulting in the fact that you would become the queen of Katyur. Then we received some shocking news—that Dulashahi had been killed in battle. You were still a child then, and I wept for the little boy you were betrothed to. Now and again we would get scraps of news—that Dharma Devi was ruling till her son grew up. I bided my time, till you began to reach marriageable age. When people began to ask us when we were going find a suitable husband for you, I reminded your father about the vow and begged him to go to Bairath, the Katyuri capital, to speak to Dharma Devi.

'"You are talking nonsense, woman," he scoffed. "Do you think the queen of Katyur will remember something that happened so long ago? She has not tried to find us or contact us after that. What if she humiliates me? I will not be able to tolerate it. Don't worry, I will arrange an equally brilliant match for our Raju." He refused to listen, no matter how much I pleaded.

'I don't know what got into his head that he always brushed my words aside. I . . . I've been so apprehensive ever since he insisted on betrothing you to the Tibetan, breaking this vow with the goddess as witness,' Ganguli ended sadly.

'Did this really happen, Ija?' Rajula's breath caught as she sat up and clasped her mother's hands. 'Oh . . . it's beyond imagination—that Malushahi was engaged to me even before we were born. No wonder I used to dream of him . . .'

'Dream?' It was her mother's turn to look startled now.

'Yes, Ija! The . . . the dreams began the day Baujyu told me that he had betrothed me to the Huniya. I swear, it's true! They were so vivid . . . and the first time I met Malushahi near the temple in Bageshwar, I couldn't believe my eyes—that the man of my dreams was actually a real person!'

'It has to be a message from the goddess!' Her mother's fingers dug into Rajula's arm through the thick sleeves of her blouse. Then her voice blurred. 'But if I tell your father, he'll never believe me.'

'If only I'd known, Ija!' Rajula cried. 'And . . . I don't think Malu knows either. So many times he asked me to marry him then and there at the temple. But I dared not agree . . . because Baujyu had already given his word. And yet, despite all my feelings of guilt, I could not bear to be parted from him. Oh, what should we do now? If only Chitrashila Devi would help us.'

There was a long anguished pause. Then her mother said slowly, 'Rajula, my child, we cannot wait for the goddess to take care of each and every problem in our lives. Sometimes we have to take matters into our own hands. There is not much time left . . .' She stroked Rajula's hands tenderly.

'Your father is making plans to get you married as soon as the weather improves.'

'Oh!' Rajula's heart plummeted. Just what she had suspected! 'If I get married, I'll never see Malu again! Why hasn't he come to take me away?'

'Who knows what holds him back . . . maybe . . . if we could send a messenger to Dharma Devi . . . But no one would dare go against your father's wishes. They . . . they all fear—'

'His magic powers . . . I know, Ija!' As her mother stared at her, startled, Rajula said accusingly, 'You hid it from me when I was a child . . . but I found out for myself.'

'I didn't want to frighten you, child!'

'I would fly there right away myself, Ija!' Rajula said, clutching her mother's hands. 'But . . .' she looked at her fearfully, 'my father's magic . . . I have a feeling someone . . . something was following me when I went to meet Malushahi. He'll catch me and drag me back.'

Ganguli was silent for a few seconds. Then she said, 'It is an impossible journey, Raju. How will you travel all alone through those dense forests? You're just a young, vulnerable girl. Not only wild animals, but also many other perils lie on the way: spirits and demons that haunt lonely paths and evil men who waylay travellers. Even a well-armed man would hesitate.'

'If that is so, Ija, there's nothing to do but resign myself to my fate, and . . . and . . . you can face the consequences of breaking your vow.' Rajula lay down on the bed with a jerk, turning her back on her mother. Why did Ija keep telling her to keep hoping and then discourage her?

There was a long silence, punctuated only by the sound of Rajula's agitated breathing. Then Ganguli spoke, 'Either way, we stand to suffer,' she said slowly. 'Maybe it is better to act. I think . . . it is possible to escape your father's notice. He's not so suspicious now. You have been so obedient all this while that he's confident you've learnt your lesson. And . . . tomorrow he departs on a journey—to finalize your wedding plans, I suspect. If you have to go to Bairath, it's the best time. Also . . . you might be angry that I never told you earlier, but I know a few magic tricks myself, which could protect you during your journey. But, Raju, you must leave soon, before the dark phase of the moon begins. Follow the stars as I tell you and you will not lose your way.' Her mother's eyes suddenly gleamed in the darkness.

'Oh, Ija!' Rajula hugged her. 'I knew you would find a way!'

8

A Perilous Journey Begins

Rajula hurried through the forest. Leaving home had been far simpler than she had expected. Just as Ija had told her, her father had saddled his horse the next morning, loaded a few pack animals, and set off up the rocky mountain path that led towards the border of Tibet. Some of his attendants accompanied him.

'Rajula, do not forget you are promised in marriage. You must not leave your mother's side even for a moment.' His voice had been low but his frown menacing, as he swung himself onto his horse. 'Remember, nothing remains hidden from me.'

Rajula shrank back as he jerked the reins to hold the restless horse down. Could he have guessed their plans? Or worse—read their thoughts? Her heart thumped so loudly that she was terrified he might hear. She lowered her eyes as she replied in a tremulous whisper, 'I will,

Baujyu, I'll try to do as you wish. I pray you may have a safe journey.'

'Take good care of our daughter, Rajula's mother,' he turned to Ganguli. His voice had softened a bit, but the stern note underlying it could not be ignored.

'As you say, Rajula's father,' her mother replied meekly. 'May you travel without harm, by the grace of Lord Ganesha.'

They had both stood and watched the small group wind up the slope. When the tinkle of the animals' bells began to fade as did the low voices of the men chanting mantras to ensure no dangers plagued their journey, they both turned homeward, trying to ignore the stares of the curious who had gathered.

Planning the journey took up the whole day. They had to speak in low voices, in case the helpers—the women who helped with the domestic chores, the men who took care of their horses and other animals—overheard them. Only when the sky dimmed and they finished their usual early evening meal was it safe. When all the helpers had returned to their homes in the village, and the one man who lived in the quarters nearby had retired, her mother had closed the door and brought out the sharp knife she used to cut the strands of wool while weaving. Rajula gnawed at her fingers as Ija turned towards a wall in their bedroom and carefully traced a circle on it with the knife, then carved it deeper and deeper.

Her eyes widened as her mother loosened the round plug of mud plaster and detached it to reveal a hollow space. An earthen pot lay inside. She suppressed a gasp as Ganguli removed a small leather bag from it.

'What's all this?' Rajula whispered. The look of intense concentration on Ija's face unnerved her.

'Wait and see . . .' Ganguli fished around in the bag, took out a square silver locket, and opened it gently.

As Rajula gaped at the grey powder inside it, her mother's grave eyes met hers. 'There's charmed ash inside this amulet,' she said. 'It'll protect you from harm.' A faint smile brightened her face as she said dreamily, 'A mere pinch can transform you into any form you wish to take–animal, bird or insect.'

'What?' Rajula's eyes widened with astonishment.

'Yes, that's what I was told and I have no reason to disbelieve it. Just repeat these words before you open it.'

'Chhoo-mantar-chhoo
Chhoo-mantar-chhoo!
Ash of magic
Do your work, do!
In a trice
Turn me into . . .'

Rajula's face tingled as she repeated the words hesitantly. Could those nonsensical sounding words really have that effect?

'Do you want to test it, Raju?' her mother startled her. 'Try it! But chant the words slowly and carefully, or it will not work.'

Rajula hesitated. The thought of taking on an animal shape was sickening, somehow. And what about the risk? Suppose she could not return to her own self, and was forced to always stay a hairy pig, or a snarling wolf, or a creepy-crawly spider? Ugh. But . . . I need this protection, she thought, sighing. She forced herself to take the pinch of ash from her mother, with shaky fingers. The charm stuck in her throat as she repeated it slowly in a quavering voice. What did she want to turn into? Of course, a dove, one of those pretty little birds who could be heard cooing, '*Ghughuti, ghughuti!*' over and over again. So feeling rather silly, she said, 'Turn me into a *ghughuti* . . .'

It happened! What a shock to turn into a tiny creature hopping on the ground, craning her neck to look up at her mother. How scarily large she appeared!

Rajula's arms and legs had vanished, and instead of skin she was covered with feathers. Could she move, fly? She hopped awkwardly on her bird feet and hesitantly flapped her wings. Yes, she could fly! She rose into the air and took a couple of fluttery rounds of the room before settling on her mother's outstretched hand. Ija stroked her gently before saying, 'You have to chant it once more to return to your original form.'

Rajula blinked, opened and closed her beak. 'You haven't lost your human speech, my child!' Ija smiled.

Cautiously Rajula chanted the spell. Her voice felt alien, with its low, throbbing tone.

It worked.

Within seconds she had shed her feathers and wings, and regained her smooth skin, her long hair, the arms and legs she had been born with. It was an indescribable sensation. She felt large and unwieldy, but relieved—how relieved! 'Ija!' she cried, running a wondering hand down her arm. 'Did it really happen? I feel as if I'm dreaming.'

'I saw it with my own eyes,' Ija patted her cheek. 'Raju, my child . . . I have held on to these charms for years, kept them safe. I never imagined that they would come in use this way.'

'But . . . but from where did you get them, Ija?' Rajula demanded.

Her mother's eyes flickered away. She took a few moments to reply. 'When I didn't have a child for many years, I went to an old aunt, a very wise woman known to have special powers. I begged her to help me. We longed to have a family, and as you know, not having a child is considered a great sorrow for a woman, and for her husband as well. Kaki said, "I have no magic for your condition, my child—only Chitrashila Devi can help you.

Go to her temple and pray." As I rose disheartened, she continued, "I cannot let a daughter return empty-handed, however. Take these; they will not help you in this problem, but could come in handy in other ways. Only . . . do not use them unless it's a desperate situation. Magic should not be employed for frivolous reasons, or to harm anyone. Never forget that." She gave me a few simple objects and taught me the mantras that go with them. When I returned, I hid them here in the wall. I was a little frightened and almost hoped I wouldn't need them. Still it was comforting, empowering, in fact, to possess my own magic charms, like your father has his.'

'Does . . . does Baujyu know?'

Ganguli shook her head. 'Kaki said it should be a secret till I needed them urgently.' She let out a little laugh. 'Frankly, I half believed and half disbelieved. That's why I wanted to try them out before you left.'

'Oh, Ija!' Rajula still felt dazed. She froze, not daring to breathe as her mother tied the amulet around her neck. It felt cold and heavy, almost suffocating.

A perfume case came next. It was amazingly similar to the one that hung from her mother's waist. Ganguli opened it just a chink, put a hand on Rajula's head and muttered some words. 'This is special attar,' she said. 'Whoever inhales it will fall asleep instantly. The spell I've repeated will protect you from its effects.'

Rajula gazed at her, awestruck. Never in her wildest

dreams could she have imagined that her quiet mother had all these extraordinary magical objects hidden away.

'One more little thing,' Ija said. She unrolled a crumpled piece of cloth and removed a gnarled and twisted root. 'This is very helpful, too.' She flung it to the ground, hissing out the words:

'Sh-sh-show yourself
Come out of your shell, do!
Sarp Deva,
All-powerful Lord of Snakes,
We need your help, we do!'

Rajula suppressed a shriek when she heard an answering hiss. Her hair stood on end as she found a real snake writhing on the ground near her feet!

'Please, Ija,' she began, but her mother was already intoning, with folded hands:

'We thank you much,
We thank you so,
Blessed Sarp Deva,
Into your shell
Return now, please go!'

And within seconds the snake shrivelled into a dirty yellow root again.

'Where shall we hide this?' her mother wrinkled her broad brow. 'I know!' She quickly loosened Rajula's tightly braided hair.

'Not in my hair, Ija!'

'Child, it's the safest place. No one will find it and you can pull it out easily when you need it. Remember, it won't change shape till you ask it to. Now learn the spells by heart silently while I do this.'

Deftly, Ganguli twisted the root into her daughter's long, black plait. Rajula went over the strange words again and again in her head.

'You're almost ready,' her mother said when she was done. She wrapped the *kaamla*, a black blanket-like shawl, tightly around Rajula's body, securing it at her waist with a cummerband. 'The nights are still very cold,' she said. 'Keep your head well covered.' She draped another shawl over her ears, a soft pashmina she had woven especially for Rajula's trousseau. 'And you will need some money, too,' she added. 'Here, keep these silver *tankas*. Put them in your shoes for safety.' The fluttering in Rajula's belly became unbearable as her mother counted out the coins. She had never done anything like this in her life.

Then she handed her a bundle of food for the journey, some *sattu*—the roasted barley flour they carried on their travels, strips of dried goat meat and a few chapattis, tied up in a piece of cloth. Rajula hoisted it on her back along with the change of clothes she was carrying in a bag.

'Wait,' Ija whispered, as Rajula took a nervous step forward. Ija opened the door and peered out, then took a deep breath and muttered a few words, to ensure a safe journey for Rajula. She paused for a while as if listening, then said, 'Come.'

Rajula almost stumbled over the threshold.

'It's all right now,' Ija murmured, embracing Rajula. 'Go safely, my child.'

Rajula clung to her for a moment, then looked left and right. There was nothing to be heard except the monotonous chirrup of the crickets.

The whole household was in the grip of a deep slumber. Even the alert watchdogs slept soundly for once.

Rajula looked back at her mother one last time, then walked swiftly into the shadows. Her heart thudded as she broke into a run, trying to get away from the village as fast she could. A dog barked somewhere, making her speed her steps. Only when she was within the relative safety of the forest did she slow her stride.

She flung a quick glance at the sky. Her mother had told her which stars would guide her on her journey. She had to travel south, to Malushahi's capital—the city of Bairath.

9

The Secrets of the Forest

The moonlight sieved through the scattered trees, relieving the darkness, and only the constant chatter of the crickets and the occasional howl of a jackal broke the utter silence. Rajula's breath came quick as she hurried on. It almost felt like another dream. She was so preoccupied with watching the path that she had to remind herself she going to meet her beloved Malu. Oh, if only she could speed to him right away!

She fingered the amulet at her throat, tempted to change herself into a swift flying bird so she could soar over the trees and reach much faster than she would on foot. With an effort she controlled herself, recalling what her mother had said–that the charm should only be used when it was urgently needed. No, she had to exercise caution. Who knew what might lie ahead? Remembering her father, she shivered. Had he left any of his captive spirits behind to watch over her? Almost reflexively she turned to glance behind her, peered up at the trees to see if some telltale rags of mist were draped over them.

Where was he now? Had he reached Hundesh already? It was supposed to be a long, arduous trek and no one attempted it in this season. There was too much snow blocking the passes. But people believed Sunapati Shauka possessed the power to sail over the highest of peaks.

She drew a deep breath, taking in the piquant scent of the junipers, which mingled with that of the herbs below her feet—wild caraway, thyme and catmint. The occasional silver birch trees loomed like slender apparitions. It was the first time in her life that she was going anywhere, absolutely alone. After all those months of torturous confinement it was exhilarating. She felt as carefree as a butterfly flitting about unrestrained, flying anywhere she wished.

As her feet sped her down the slopes, her thoughts flew back to the day she had been joking and laughing with her friends on their journey to Bageshwar. How much had changed since then! So much had happened to her—meeting Malushahi, incurring her father's wrath. She felt as if she were someone different now, not the same Rajula whose only worry had been to finish her chores fast enough to be able to go out and play with her friends, who had been so bitterly disappointed when the wild berries she loved were plundered by hungry bears.

The thought of bears evoked a tiny shudder. The low shrubs of the higher slopes had given way to a forest of the coniferous *raga* trees. There might be some bears prowling here. Leopards, too. And what about the ghosts, demons and fairies that were said to appear at night?

Barely had the thought entered her head when the strains of distant music came to her ears. Someone playing a flute in the middle of the night in this lonely forest? Was she imagining it? She halted for a moment to listen carefully. The sound, faint though it was, was unmistakable. Rajula drew the shawl closer around her head. Without warning, the night had turned so chilly that her teeth were chattering.

Her felt boots were quite soundless on the thick covering of deodar needles that carpeted the forest floor. However, Rajula slowed her pace to tread even more softly. The music grew louder. Suddenly an overpowering urge possessed her. She had never heard anything so enthralling . . . it was calling her . . . she had to go closer to it!

Even as her feet carried her on, a thought tugged at her and goose bumps pricked her arms. This music . . . she had heard about it . . . An uncontrollable shiver ran through her frame . . .

This is stupid, she scolded herself, I'll never get to Bairath if I start trembling because of a silly flute. Determinedly, she tried to shut the sound out and tramp on. But without any warning, the dense forest thinned into a clearing.

Rajula halted with a start.

The moonlight picked out a strange scene. Two men stood there, one playing a flute, the other keeping time with a *hurka* drum, while women decked out in shimmering gossamer garments danced. They were more beautiful than any mortal could be—their ethereal features, large glowing eyes . . . the way they moved, fluidly, as if they did not possess a single bone in their bodies. An eerie phosphorescence surrounded them. Or was it that the moon shone more brightly on this spot?

Rajula stood there, transfixed. Were they *ancharies*, the fairies that appeared at night? No, they looked like *apsaras* that had come down from the court of Lord Indra himself, she mused. Then these must be the two wizard brothers, Sidua and Bidua Ramol, talked about in the stories of her village. No one could play the flute more beautifully, she'd been told, and that their music was so beguiling that it even enticed the *apsaras* away from heaven.

Rajula went on listening, mesmerized—it was as if someone was pouring the coolest silver into her ears. Then she realized that, unknowingly, she had stepped out of the forest into the clearing. She didn't know when and how the dancing fairies surrounded her; she just found herself there among them, trying to follow their movements. The most melodious song she had ever heard was throbbing in her veins, lifting her arms, making them whirl and twirl, forcing her feet to step to its rhythm. It was so captivating that she forgot everything else. Forgot her quest, the reason for her being in the forest at this unearthly hour.

All she wanted was to remain there dancing to that heavenly music forever.

Suddenly an owl's mournful hoot pierced through the veil of song: *Whoo–too-whoo-too whoo!* Rajula's feet halted, her arms dropped. She looked around, confused. What was happening? She shrank away from the fairies, hugging herself, cold and afraid. And then the words of the song that was wrapping round her like an enchanted web began to become clearer and clearer.

A current jolted through Rajula. The heavenly creatures, whoever they were, were singing:

'A bride, a bride, a lovely bride
For Sidua, a lovely bride . . .
Bring jewels and gold
For Sidua's bride,
Garments of velvet and silk,
A silver palanquin to carry her off–
Sidua's lovely bride . . .'

She could see Sidua advancing towards her, his pale skin glowing, his green eyes jewel bright. The fairies were so close that their robes were brushing against her, and the heady fragrance that wafted out from them was making her dizzy.

She felt a terrible tug. How she wanted to succumb to their overwhelming charm, to let them carry her away . . .

Just then, the owl hooted again, breaking the spell. Rajula shook her head hard to snap out of the trance. What was she doing here? She was on her way to Bairath. But as she tried to move away, the fairies closed up. They were chanting: *A bride for Sidua! A bride for Sidua!*

The words swirled around her, faster and faster. Rajula clutched her forehead, tried to steady her wavering feet. She was trapped! How could she get out? As if in answer, her mother's voice echoed in her ear. Somehow, she pulled herself together and tugged at the root in her hair. She flung it down, repeated the spell and soon an enormous snake was squirming on the ground.

The effect was instantaneous. The fairies shrieked and flew off in different directions like a swarm of large dragonflies scattering. Sidua's silver flute dropped from his hands. He and his brother fled after the fairies. Hurriedly, Rajula chanted the reverse mantra and the snake became a root again. She scooped it off the ground, tucked it back into her hair and fled back into the forest. For a few minutes she leaned against a tree, panting, trembling, trying to gather her wits. Then she gazed up at the stars to get her bearings, and set off again.

10

A Game of Wits

Rajula didn't know how her feet sped on so swiftly. It was as if they had a life of their own as they leapt over rocks, zigzagged through trees and bushes, scurried uphill and downhill. They wound down on their own, too, as if they sensed she had put a safe distance between herself and the wizards and fairies. She slowed her pace and walked on steadily. But after a couple of hours she began to weary. And the stars were dimming in the sky; soon they would not be visible, making it hard for her to keep on track. Maybe it was time to rest. She glanced around, and after rejecting a couple of possibilities, found the perfect spot. Dense bushes huddled together in a small circle—a natural hiding place. Rolling herself up in her shawl, she stretched out. Within seconds she was fast asleep.

Bright rays of sunlight pierced her eyelids, forcing them to open. Rajula sat up with a start. For a few moments she was confused, wondering why she was here, sleeping in the woods. Had she taken the goats to pasture and dozed off? Then she recalled that she had not done that for a long time. Not since she had encountered Malushahi and had been forcibly separated from him. Sudden elation fizzed up, as she remembered her mission. Then, as her thoughts sped through the events of the night, she shuddered. What if the owl had not hooted? And if she had not been carrying her mother's magic charms? Would she have become a captive again, as Sidua's bride?

However, she had to move on.

How long had she slept? The sun was already high in the sky. She sprang to her feet. It was a wonderful morning in the month of Jyeshtha and the mild fragrance of the *kunj*, the wild rose and other wildflowers came to her. Where was she? According to her observations she should have covered at least a quarter, if not one-third, of the distance to Bairath.

The soothing sound of flowing water reached her ears. How fortunate, a stream nearby! She could have a wash, drink some water. Rushing through the night, no thought of food and drink had entered her head.

As she splashed cold water on her face, she tried to recall the landmarks her mother had mentioned, which would keep her on the right way to Bairath. Then she pulled out her bundle of food and began to eat some of the roasted barley flour she was carrying.

She would have to be careful, she thought as she munched, avoid villages and any stray person she glimpsed, lest people inquire why she, a girl, was roaming around all alone.

And then, she heard another sound, which made her groan inwardly. She quickly swallowed a mouthful, took a drink of water and prepared to run.

A man's voice, humming tunelessly. Not enticing at all, unlike the music that had captivated her last night. Any human voice was a threat, to be scrupulously avoided. She tied up her bundle of *sattu* and hurried up the rocky path that led up from the stream. She was trying to decide which direction to take when a man emerged from behind a thicket of trees.

Short, bow-legged, with untidy hair poking out from beneath his conical cap. He wore a long, greyish, wraparound coat and narrow white trousers. A stout pole was slung across his shoulders and stacked pots were hanging from it. Rajula guessed he was a yoghurt seller from the nearby town of Doonagiri, famous for its dairy products. This meant she was near Dwarahat, not too far from Malushahi's capital, Bairath.

She was poised to dart into the cover of the trees, when the man caught sight of her.

'*Hunh!*' he grunted, as he stopped to stare at her long and hard.

Rajula folded her hands, bowed her head politely and said, 'Namaskar, Kaka.'

She tried to walk past him briskly, hoping he would not insist on engaging her in conversation.

The man's brow furrowed. 'May you live long. Wait, wait, what's the hurry? What are you doing here all alone?'

'I . . . I'm grazing my goats,' Rajula said. It was the first thing that came to her mind, and she realized right away that it would not work.

'Goats? I can't see any goats? Not a single one!'

When Rajula made no reply, he looked her up and down again. A smile split his face, revealing a mouthful of crooked yellow teeth. 'A lovely young girl, all alone in the forest! Don't you know it's not safe?' Very deliberately he put the pole and the pots down, and leaned towards her, speaking in a conspiratorial tone: 'Have you run away from home? Or maybe you have no family . . . or you have a stepmother who ill-treats you? *Hanh*, is that so?'

'No, no, Kaka, my parents live in the village nearby,' Rajula said at once.

'Now, now, you're not telling the truth. I know everyone in the next village and the next. And you don't seem to be from these parts. Tell me why you're all alone. I can help you.'

'I don't need help,' Rajula said abruptly. She should run, she thought, but the man might chase her.

'You don't have to hide anything from me. You're obviously too innocent to know what dangers lie ahead for a young girl on her own. See, I'm a decent man. And it's an honourable man's duty to offer protection to a girl like you.'

'You are most kind, Kaka.' Rajula folded her hands. 'But I'm in a hurry. I'm actually going to my sister's village.'

The man shook his head. 'No one would send a girl unescorted. Now just listen—I, Fachua Doyarva, am offering you an excellent opportunity to lead a respectable life. I'm in need of a wife—you look like a healthy girl, apart from being quite pretty. I will marry you and I promise you will live in luxury. Hardly any work—just eight cowsheds to clean and eight bundles of grass to cut each day. You can bask in the sun the rest of the day.' When Rajula remained silent, he continued, 'And I'm really strong, too! See?'

He picked up one of the heavy bronze pots he was carrying and pressed it between his hands. To Rajula's astonishment, it collapsed into a shapeless mass of metal.

'See?' he repeated with a smug smile. 'You won't find a stronger man than me.'

Rajula was a little taken aback at the feat. Alarmed, too. This man would not let her go easily, she knew now. Irritation flushed her cheeks. Why did each and every man she met on the way want to marry her?

How would she get rid of him . . .

She smiled as sweetly as she could. 'That's very kind of you, to offer me—a helpless girl all alone—protection!

But . . . there is a particular custom in Jalnar Desh—from where I come. A prospective groom has to prove his skill at dancing.'

'Is that all? I'm a very accomplished dancer, you know—quite famous in my village. Let me show you the buffalo dance. Watch!'

Fachua tied a piece of cloth around his waist, put a hand on his hips and began to waggle them and twirl round and round, humming tunelessly again.

Rajula hid her smile and began to clap to the beat. All the time, her mind was whirling—how could she escape?

Fachua stopped and said, 'I can do even better. Shall I show you the lion dance?'

Rajula wrinkled her nose. '*Oh-ho!* People may praise your dancing here. But . . . can you dance upside down? That's the real test of a good dancer in my land.'

'Is that a joke?'

'No, no! I mean it! Why would I joke?'

Fachua narrowed his eyes at Rajula again, then frowned. 'Are you sure you're not pulling my leg?'

'Why should I, Kaka, when you're trying to help me?'

'Hmm . . . but stop calling me Kaka. I'm not your uncle. I can't be . . . We are going to get married, remember!' He threw another suspicious glance at her, then said, 'Well . . . I'm no less than those fellows from your land. Personally, I think it's a silly idea, but it's the easiest thing in the world.

I'm a very agile fellow, you know. Now you just watch. Your eyes will pop out in amazement!'

Fachua flung himself on the ground and tried to swing his stubby frame into the air, but failed to keep his balance. Rajula groaned inwardly as he flopped to the ground.

'Hmm . . . normally I can do it in a jiffy,' he grinned. 'Never mind, here goes–*uhhh!*'

Again he dropped to the ground. Rajula clenched her teeth. What would happen if he weren't able to do it?

'Try again,' she said encouragingly. 'You almost managed it last time!'

Fachua simply nodded as he dusted his hands and dove to the ground. Rajula held her breath as he tried to fling his legs into the air and straighten them. He wobbled for a while, then she sighed with relief when he managed to maintain the posture.

And as Rajula watched, trying to suppress her giggles, he began to spin around cautiously, then wave his legs in the air, as he grew more confident.

The moment he turned his face the other way, she quickly removed the long white *pichhaura* she had tied around her head for the sake of convenience, instead of letting it hang loose, and draped it over the stump of a rhododendron tree. Then fingering her amulet, she chanted the mantra. Within seconds she had turned into a flea, barely visible to the eye. She hopped off as fast as she could, pausing only once to throw a quick backward glance to see what was happening behind her. The breeze was filling out the *pichhaura*, keeping it fluttering gently. Fachua continued to dance upside down, blissfully unaware that she had gone.

His words came to her ear faintly. 'I'm good, aren't I, girl? Come on, admit it!'

Rajula just hopped on faster!

11

The Edge of Disaster

Rajula perched on the leaf of a *kilmori* bush and muttered the spell. Then she screamed as long thorns punctured her arms. The transformation was so sudden that she had lost her balance and fallen into the bush. More pricks assailed her as she got to her feet somehow and scrambled out of the bush. Returning to her human shape was a mixed blessing, she thought! For a moment she shivered, feeling exposed and vulnerable again. But her mother had warned her not to stay in the animal form longer than was necessary.

A deep sigh tore out of her chest. What else would she have to do to get to Malushahi? The episode had jolted her, coming so soon after the first. If only she had known that it would be so dangerous for a girl on her own . . . It would not have stopped her, but she would have tried to be more careful.

She had also lost time. To make up she trekked on rapidly, not stopping except for a quick drink whenever she found a spring. Fortunately she did not meet anyone on the way as she walked on and on. But when the shadows began to lengthen, the prospect of continuing through the night made her heart sink. It was a knotty choice. The stars were the best guide. During the day she had to search for the landmarks her mother had mentioned, the sight of a particular hill to identify a location, or a river flowing downhill to show her that she was going south as she needed to.

What should she do? The soles of her feet were sore and tender, and her legs felt like two heavy logs she had to struggle to drag along. Should she rest for a while? The sight of a narrow cave opening up in the hillside decided her. It looked like the ideal place to take a short nap. She clambered up the slope and peeped in cautiously, shuddering as the memory of that other cave surfaced. This one was empty and seemed reasonably clean, only the opening was extremely cramped. Maybe that made it safer. Rajula crawled in slowly. A musty smell greeted her, but it was not too overpowering. Gratefully, she stretched out on the bare ground. And within minutes she was sound asleep.

She woke to the sound of birdcall. Again, it took her a few moments to recall where she was. She banged her head so hard on the roof of the cave as she sat up that tears sprang out of her eyes. There was nothing to do, however, but drop to her hands and knees, and edge towards the entrance. When she peeped out she noticed that the darkness was beginning to dissolve and the outlines of the trees were clearly visible. She had slept through the night, lost valuable time! The stars that were to guide her might have faded from the sky. She would have to rely on the landmarks. But a good night's rest had refreshed her.

She crept out warily. There was no movement to be seen anywhere, except for the branches of the trees swaying in the breeze. No sight of anyone who might pose a threat. Perhaps it was too early. As she ran down the hillside, the cold air bit her cheeks, and an occasional gust of wind made her shiver. The cave had been quite snug. She wrapped her shawl around her head and pressed on.

Soon the sun came up, warming Rajula's stiff frame, lifting her mood. Briskly, she strode on, humming a tune to pass the way.

Half the day had gone by when, as she was hurrying down a narrow path, she glimpsed a cluster of slate roofs. Terraced fields stretched below them. A small village? The sight of a broad river winding through the fields made her shriek in excitement. She was quite close to Bairath!

She had to, however, bypass the village. Also, she was quite exhausted again. Her legs ached and her throat was parched. It was quite some time since she'd chanced upon a spring. She glanced around, looking for the usual signs—extra greenery, dampness on the ground. Then a faint scent of moist earth came to her. A hurried search yielded a narrow brook, gushing through mossy ground, past a thicket of leafy trees.

Rajula bent and gulped down handful after handful of the crystal-clear water. She splashed it on her face, savouring its earthy scent. Then she sank to the ground and dangled her throbbing feet in the narrow channel to soothe them. As the icy water ran over her feet, her exhaustion drained away.

Suddenly her stomach rumbled. She tore her bundle of food open and gobbled up several mouthfuls of *sattu*, then chewed on a piece of dried meat. It felt perfect—sitting there, listening to the humming of the bees and the distant birdcalls. And, very soon she would meet Malu! She chuckled as she thought of how she had fooled both Sidua and Fachua, and when she visualized Fachua searching for her, she burst into a fit of giggling.

As she sat there lost in thoughts of Malushahi, she didn't notice that two men were gaping at her wide-eyed. This little stream was actually an irrigation channel two brothers, Lachchhi and Bachchi Mahara, had diverted from a spring to water their fields. When the flow of water suddenly slackened, their servants had came to find out what was obstructing it.

The astonished men gazed at Rajula for a while, then crept away, baffled.

'What's the matter?' Lachchhi Mahara called out when they reached the fields. 'What's blocking the flow? Did you find out?'

The two servants looked at each other, scratched their heads and smiled sheepishly. 'Can't you speak?' Bachchi yelled. The brothers were notorious for their temper. 'Has someone sewn up your mouths?'

'No, no, Dada!' The older of the servants spoke. 'There . . . there's a woman sitting there . . . with her feet in the channel.'

'So? Why didn't you tell her to go away? Or are you scared of a mere woman?'

'No! Dada, no! It's not that . . .'

Before he could say anything further, the other servant burst out. 'Don't know if it's a woman or some heavenly being! *Babba-ho!* She looks too beautiful to be real. That's why we didn't dare say anything.'

'You stupid fellows have lost your minds.' Lachchhi aimed a cuff at the man's head. 'What would heavenly beings be doing here in broad daylight? Come, Bachchi, let's go and check up ourselves. These no-good fellows can't be trusted to do anything.'

Cursing and laughing, the brothers clambered up the slope towards the stream. When they got close they both stopped in their tracks too, dumbstruck.

'The fools were right,' Lachchhi muttered. 'She is stunning.'

'Yes, Lachchhi, for once you are right, too,' Bachchi stepped forward. 'I . . . I think I would be very happy to marry a girl like this one.'

At that very moment Rajula looked up. When she set eyes on two large, hairy men advancing towards her, she sprang to her feet, alarmed. But by that time Bachchi had reached close enough to grab her arm.

'No, you don't!' cried his brother. 'I saw her first. And I'm older than you. Let go! I'm going to marry her.' He caught hold of her other arm.

'Certainly not! I claimed her first. She's mine!' Bachchi tried to pull Rajula away.

'No! She's mine!' cried Lachchhi, dragging her towards him.

'Stop! Please stop! You're hurting me!' Rajula cried out. 'Let go of me!'

But the brothers wouldn't stop. They kept screaming and yelling at each other, tugging Rajula this way and that, almost pulling her arms out.

'Help! Please help! Save me, someone!' Rajula screamed at the top of her voice. 'Let go! Please let go!' She struggled to shake them off, but the brothers held on tighter.

Her screams and their shouts soon attracted a crowd. All the people working in the fields—men, women and children—rushed towards them to see what was happening.

'Help me!' Rajula called out. 'Tell them to let me go!'

For a moment there was only the rumble of numerous voices talking together. People called out to the brothers, 'Leave her be!' 'Let the girl go!' but they ignored them.

A man even stepped forward, then halted as one of the brothers growled menacingly. 'Stay away! This is between us two!'

They were beginning to pull Rajula this way and that again when an authoritative voice rasped out, 'Stop! Leave the girl alone.'

It was an old man leaning on a stick. Though he was bent and his face cobwebbed with wrinkles, his eyes gleamed fiercely from beneath his shaggy white brows. To Rajula's surprise and relief, the two quarrelling brothers dropped her arms and stood there sheepishly. She rubbed her aching arms and surreptitiously fingered her amulet, thought of the root in her hair. But there were too many people around. If by chance her charm did not work, they might think she was a witch and treat her worse. How could she get away? Then she noticed a small snake coiled around the old man's wrist and turned cold with fright. All thoughts of escape vanished.

'Fools,' the old man said sternly, 'you're ready to kill yourself over a woman. There is a better way to decide.'

Lachchhi was the first to speak. 'Mamjyu . . . what . . . what brings you here?' he stuttered.

'I, Nagimal, may live deep down in Nagalok, the land of snakes, but I keep an eye on you fellows. When I saw what you were up to, I had to rush here.'

Rajula's eyes widened. An uncle who was a *naga*! Thankfully there was someone they feared.

'Go and prepare a meal, each of you. Then serve the food in a *thali* and offer it to the girl. The one whose *thali* she touches first will marry her. And you come with me, girl, while they're doing that.'

Rajula glanced around desperately. But there were still too many people around for her to employ her magic.

She slumped in a corner of the small dark room they ushered her into. The formidable old man squatted near the door, glancing at her now and again as he kept watch. Rajula's head throbbed in despair. How could she get away?.

The meal took a long time to prepare. Delicious aromas wafted to her. She could smell the most fragrant rice cooking. After living on *sattu* for two days, it seemed heavenly. Then the sharp tang of red chillies pricked her nostrils. The sweet scent of cinnamon came as a relief, and the more robust one of bay leaves sizzling in the purest ghee. Her famished stomach rumbled. But she was well aware that this was one meal she could not afford to even taste.

The brothers were vying with each other to dish up the choicest fare. While Lachchhi had got hold of the freshest fish from the river Rahap that flowed close by, Bachchi was able to corner a pot of the creamiest yoghurt from Doonagiri. Both sent their servants out for the plumpest and most delicious bananas, as well as the most scrumptious of sweets to entice Rajula. While one of them made *kheer*, the other decided to lure her with *halwa*.

Finally two platters were filled with all the delicacies the brothers had prepared. And the two approached Rajula, scowling at each other.

'See what I've got, my lovely,' Lachchhi said, thrusting his platter under her nose. He smiled, showing small, stained teeth. 'You could never have tasted anything like this in your life. Can you scent the spices in this curry made from the tender flesh of a young goat?'

'He's got peasant's fare, nothing compared to what I'm offering,' Bachchi sneered, as he presented his meal. 'My fish is far superior.'

'Careful! If you drop my food, I'll teach you a lesson!'

'What lesson?'

'Quiet!' Nagimal thundered. 'Hurry up, girl!'

Rajula looked at the two heaped platters. How tempting both looked! With a huge effort she controlled the pangs of hunger that were turning her faint. Resolutely, she stretched her arms out and quickly touched both at the same time, saying, 'Thank you, Bubu, thank you, Kaka!'

The crowd of onlookers who were standing there waiting for her decision with bated breath, exploded into laughter.

'She called you grandfather, Bachchi, and you uncle, Lachchhi! It's clear she wants neither of you!' A man called out. 'And I don't blame her.'

'What a clever girl!' someone else remarked. 'She kept you working half the day and outwitted both of you!'

'I'll show you how clever she is!' Lachchhi howled, throwing down the *thali*.

'And I will, too!' Bachchi chimed in, letting his drop, too.

Before anyone could react, they pounced on Rajula and pulled her away.

'Clever, are you?' Lachchhi cried. 'I'll show you what clever is!'

'I'm your grandfather, am I?' Bachchi shrieked.

They dragged her off, ignoring their uncle's admonitions to be gentle, ignoring the villagers' outrage. When they were alone on the banks of the river, they beat her mercilessly till she slumped to the ground, out cold.

For a moment they stood there staring at her. Then Lachchhi said in a low voice, 'Is she dead?'

'No . . . I can see her breathing,' Bachchi replied after a few moments. 'Shall we fling her into the river? She deserves it!'

Lachchhi stared at the ground. 'Why take the sin of murder on your head?' he said. 'Let's shut her up in a wooden box and throw her into the river. Her destiny will decide whether she lives or dies.'

'At least she'll be gone from here, the minx.'

Rajula lay there helplessly. There was no way she could resist. She well knew it would be a mistake to; it would be better to just play unconscious. But as they flung her into the box and the lid slammed down on her ominously, her heart plummeted to its lowest ebb. Terrified, she passed out.

The box floated along the river.

Rajula didn't know how long it was when she came to her senses. She beat frantically at the lid of the box, hoping to force it open. It only made her already sore arms ache worse. A terrible fear wrapped around her like a blanket of ice. Was she going to die here, either suffocating in the box or drowning in the river? Would she never meet her Malu again? Why couldn't people leave her alone? To travel all this distance, just to die like this!

Her grief overcame her so that she began to wail loudly saying, 'O Baghnath! You are responsible for my plight! Why did you grant my wish only to separate me from Malu? What cruel game are you playing with me? I have never done anyone any harm. Why do I have to suffer this way?'

She had barely finished her tirade when she was flung violently against the edge of the box. She heard a loud knock and the creak of wood splintering. What was happening? Was the god punishing her for her blasphemous words? She lay still for a moment, listening to the rapid *thud-thud-thud* of her heartbeat, waiting for what might happen next. But nothing did.

She could feel the box swaying gently beneath her and the soft lapping of waves. And suddenly a thought came to her, so exciting that she almost shrieked aloud. Could she have reached the shore?

Hesitantly, she raised an arm and pressed it against the lid of the box. To her astonishment, it gave way. Scraping up the remnants of her strength, she pushed hard with both hands and opened the lid. Eagerly she sat up.

Yes, she was close to the bank of the river. She didn't know where she was, but she had been saved! Not wasting a minute, she clambered out into the semi-darkness on to a large jagged rock. This was what the box had knocked against and this was what had broken it open!

However, she was not really out of the woods yet. She could see the bank of the river, a shadowy, tantalizing outline, a short distance away. She had to get there. Swallowing her tears of disappointment, gathering all the courage she could, Rajula slipped into the chilly water. Somehow she mustered up the strength to swim to the shore. She pulled herself onto the solid ground and lay there gasping for breath, her whole body throbbing like an open sore, without the strength to even raise her head.

Rajula did not know how the night passed, how she survived the bitter cold that seeped deep into her bones and stayed there like hard solid ice. But when the sun rose, its rays lighted on a cluster of houses and Rajula sat up, ready to go again.

She had reached the city of Bairath.

12

Bairath

Rajula's heart soared for a moment, then plummeted again. The two brothers had torn her clothes to shreds, while beating her. How could she meet Malushahi in this piteous state? He was a king. It would not be easy to get to him, looking like a destitute beggar. Who would believe that he would want to meet her! But how galling to have come so far, endured so much, and not be able to see him!

She had to find a way.

Fortunately, though they had thrown away her change of clothes, her magic charms and the silver coins her mother had given her were all intact. Food was her first and most important need; she hadn't eaten a morsel or had a sip of water for twenty-four hours and felt so starved that her legs were buckling under her like lumps of uncooked dough. Once she had eaten, she had to get hold of a set of fresh clothes. Also, she thought it might be better to wait for night to fall before trying to enter the palace.

Only . . . how could she go and buy food in this condition? And, wasn't it too early for shops to open?

As she sat there on the river bank miserably, wondering what to do, a peal of laughter clashed in her ears. The voices of women raised in animated conversation followed. Rajula sprang to her feet and prepared to run, but her legs kept folding under her. Her heart sank as she realized she would not get far, feeble as she was.

If only she could find a hiding place! Her anxiously darting eyes alighted on some bushes. Quickly, she burrowed into them.

The women came into view, tripping along jauntily, exchanging banter. They had copper pots tucked under their arms and were probably coming to the river to fetch water. A terrible pain lanced through Rajula. They looked so carefree. For a moment she longed to return to the ordinary life she had known before she set eyes on Malushahi. Gazing at the soft lines of the face of the oldest in the group, a thought wandered into her mind. Should she ask them for help? It seemed her only chance. If she waited too long, cold and wet as she was, she might fall ill and who knew who might happen to come this way next? Suppose it was someone like the two Mahara brothers? The very thought made her break out into a cold sweat. These women . . . surely they wouldn't harm her? She had to take the risk. Hesitantly, she emerged.

The first woman who saw her screamed so loudly that Rajula tottered back, startled. Was she such a terrible sight?

But the oldest asked in a gentle voice, 'What happened to you, *behni*? Are you in some kind of trouble?'

'I . . . I was treated badly by some men.' Her voice shook as she spoke. She folded her hands. 'Can you help me please, Didi? As you can see, I desperately need some clothes. Can you tell me where I can get some? I . . . I have money but cannot go anywhere in this state.'

The women sighed, shook their heads and exchanged glances. Then one of them removed the thick woollen shawl draped around her and said, 'Take this. It is big enough to cover most of you.'

The oldest woman added, 'The shops will open in a couple of hours. And if you're looking for food, there is a man selling milk close by. Just follow this path. If you need anything else . . .'

Rajula shook her head. Her eyes turned damp as she thanked them. She wrapped the shawl around her tightly, comforted by the instant warmth it brought, and passed a trembling hand over the stripes woven into it.

With hesitant steps, she plodded down the path they had indicated. Sure enough, the milkman was there. He flung a curious glance at her, but she lowered her eyes, ignoring it, as she made her request. The tall glass of the nourishing liquid went down her throat in grateful gulps, and little by little she felt strength stirring again in her listless limbs.

'How much for the milk?' she asked.

He shook her head. 'It's all right. I don't charge for just a glass.'

A lump formed in Rajula's throat. What a relief to find some good people! 'It is most kind of you,' she said. 'How . . . how do I reach the city of Bairath?'

'This path will lead you there,' he said.

Rajula's heart soared. She folded her hands in thanks and hurried on. Barely had she gone a short distance when the tempting aroma of puris frying wafted to her, reviving memories of the fair at Bageshwar. Her throat clogged up immediately.

How far she had travelled since that time! Then she had been filled with hope and joy; now she was struggling to drag herself out of the black hole of despair. No, she should not lose heart; she would not! Her fortunes had taken a turn for the better again and hopefully she would be reunited with Malushahi soon.

She walked on faster, and reached the bazaar. Following her nose, she found the shop selling food. Hunger overpowered her so that she burnt her tongue on the first crisp puri, which she gobbled hastily, along with a spicy pumpkin *sabzi* that sizzled on her tongue. The sun was beginning to show a hesitant face now and she found a spot where she could bask in its warmth for a while. What a luxury it seemed after her eventful, headlong flight! Such a comfort that soon her eyelids drooped shut on their own.

The buzz of voices accompanied by the creak of doors and the rattle of door chains jerked her awake. The shops were opening their shutters, one by one, disclosing their wares to prospective buyers. She rubbed her eyes, got to her feet and stretched, then wandered through the market, glancing around eagerly. It was tempting to let her gaze linger on all the fascinating goods on display, but she resisted the impulse till she noticed a row of *ghaghras* hanging in a stall. The usual black, a couple of coloured ones, too—a blue that seemed to have stolen colour from the midnight sky, another the deep maroon of a ripe *kaafal* berry.

Excitement was beginning to flutter within her, when a thought struck her like a chill blast. Did she have enough money? Her mother had given her fifteen silver *tankas*—the coins her father sometimes used in Tibet, though their trade was mostly by barter. She stepped aside to retrieve the money from her shoes, where she had hidden it. Then she hesitantly approached the shopkeeper.

'Dajyu,' she asked. 'How much does the blue one cost?'

The man gave her a curious glance, making her more self-conscious. She well knew she presented a strange sight, alone, obviously a stranger to the area and wrapped in a large shawl. 'It's expensive,' he said abruptly. 'Velvet with gold embroidery!'

Rajula flushed, but her mouth set stubbornly. 'How much?'

'Five silver *tankas*,' he replied, curling his lip.

'Does a blouse and *pichhaura* come with it?'

'Yes.'

The man's eyes opened wide when Rajula began to count out the coins. Then a sudden thought made her halt. She might stand out too much in that opulent outfit. 'Wait a minute,' she said.

'How much for the maroon? It's cotton–isn't it?'

'Two,' he replied sullenly.

'I'll take it.' The shopkeeper held out the *ghaghra* and the long-sleeved blouse that went with it, along with a head covering. Rajula rolled the clothes into a hasty bundle and began to search for a secluded spot to get dressed. She found it in a shady copse of oak trees, not too far from the town.

How did she look in these new clothes? No matter, at least she was properly clad. She drew a deep breath, pushing the ache at the back of her throat into some distant place. She was ready now: dressed up, well-fed and impatient to discover the city of Bairath.

The bazaar was splendid, far beyond what she could

have imagined and the variety of goods arrayed there mind-boggling.

The sight of a tall, impressive building arrested her feet. Looming over everything in the city, it was visible from afar. Her heartbeat seemed to halt. Could it be . . . ?

She turned to a passer-by, 'Is . . . is that the palace?'

'Indeed, it is. The palace of our king, Raja Malushahi. It's three storeys high. You won't find anything like it anywhere in the whole region.' The woman's admiration gleamed in her eyes. 'It's right in the middle of the city. If you want to take a closer look, take that path.' The woman pointed ahead, but Rajula had already set off!

Malushahi's palace! Rajula's breath raced like an out-of-control horse as she neared it. What a place! Surrounded by thick stone walls with intricately carved gates, it looked like a fort.

Tall, formidable-looking guards manned the entrance. Rajula's eyes almost popped out when they lighted on a large, beautifully caparisoned elephant.

Suddenly, she felt uneasy. Her hopes, her ballooning confidence began to deflate. She had not imagined such grandeur. Even if she managed to get close, would he even recall who she was? Her father's words rang in her ears—'I did not bring you up to be the plaything of kings!' Maybe he was right, he was older and knew the ways of the world better. Why would Malushahi want anything to do with her for long . . . she was, after all, just a village girl and he could marry a princess if he wanted . . . Tears scorched her eyes. Were the dreams an illusion then?

'There are seven such gates, child,' someone remarked. 'Each more splendid than the next. You have every reason to feel awestruck.' It was an old woman. A proud smile curved through her wrinkles.

Rajula gulped down her tears hastily and nodded. 'It is indeed most impressive.' With a huge effort she pulled herself together and returned the woman's smile. 'What if I wanted to meet the king?' she asked.

The woman's mouth pursed. 'You do not seem to be from these parts. Our noble king, Malushahi, is very kind, but commoners can only meet him when he holds his special durbar, once a week.'

'And will he hold it today?'

'I'm afraid it took place yesterday. You will have to wait. What is your problem?'

Rajula shook her head. 'I just wanted to find out.'

The woman looked her up and down curiously, but before she could question her further, Rajula turned and hurried away. She would definitely make an attempt to meet Malushahi. Even if he rejected her at the end. She had to find out, even if the truth dashed her hopes to the ground.

Somehow, the day went by. Rajula walked and walked, explored every nook and turn of the city, marvelling at the smoothly paved streets crowded with well-dressed people, stopping by the temples where bells never seemed to stop ringing. How different it was from her quiet village! The constant activity and the medley of sounds almost reminded her of the Bageshwar fair.

The sun had vanished, leaving a faint golden glow in the sky, and the shadows were beginning to lengthen when she started to make her way to the palace once more. As she approached, the sound of music filled the air, and she remembered what he had told her—that every evening, musicians performed in the courtyard of the palace, playing all kinds of instruments—drums, cymbals and conches as well as wind instruments like the *turi* and *ransingha*.

She sat there for a while, enjoying the music, relishing the fact that Malushahi was there inside somewhere, listening to the same melodies. If only she could meet him right away! Curbing her impatience, she decided to go and eat something. It would be much easier to make her way into the palace when everyone was fast asleep.

And then, one by one the lamps began to be extinguished in Malushahi's capital. Rajula crept along the streets, taking care to remain hidden in the shadows. She did not want to attract any undue attention—by now she knew painfully well what dangers lay in store for a girl on her own. While she was prepared to brave any peril for Malu's sake, it would be foolhardy to invite trouble and risk her mission.

The silence felt eerie. Not a sound could be heard except the occasional sharp bark of a dog or the thud of the watchmen's heavy sticks as they patrolled the city. From a safe distance, she took note of the guards at the gate of the palace. Two stood there at attention at their station, holding tall spears, accompanied by huge watchdogs, while others paced along the palace walls.

Rajula halted for a while, thinking hard, then tiptoed towards the walls and inched closer to the guards. In one swift movement she opened her perfume case and let the fragrance spread. The gentle breeze came to her aid, blowing it faster, and . . . within minutes the guards, the watchdogs, anyone within sniffing distance, had slumped into a sound sleep.

This was only the first gate, however. To reach Malushahi, she still needed to cross seven more, and eight chambers after that, but as the perfume wafted further, such a deep slumber took hold of the inhabitants of the palace that they lay as still as lifeless logs in their beds.

Nothing, no one, interrupted Rajula as she advanced through the palace, marvelling at the splendour she found all around her. It felt like another wonderful dream. The beautifully carved doors and pillars, the hangings of pure silk, the intricately painted murals on the walls—gods and goddesses, birds and animals, sacred patterns and motifs. But how would she find Malushahi's bedchamber? She grew impatient as she hurried along opening doors, peeping inside. A few women were sprawled this way and that here. An old man huddled inside his covers, snoring loudly.

Not this one. Not that. Why did his palace possess so many rooms? Would the charm last long enough? Panic quickened her heartbeat. Then, as she paused, exasperated, outside yet another door, she heard a sigh, and a murmur . . .

'Rajula . . .'

A current thrilled through her frame. She had found him! And he had not forgotten her! Was he dreaming of her?

She pushed the door open and ran in. Her eyelids pricked with tears as she saw him stretched out in his silver-framed bed. This was the moment she had been waiting for so long!

'Malu,' she whispered, 'I'm here, Malu, your Rajula has come.' He stirred again and muttered something. 'Wake up,' she said urgently, 'wake up! I'm here!'

Malushahi, however, remained sound asleep.

Rajula longed to shake him awake. But how could she treat him so roughly? After gazing at him uncertainly for a while, she sat down at the foot of his bed and began to tickle his left foot gently. Malu did not seem to feel it at all. She stroke his foot, harder and harder, pinched it, then tugged at his toes.

Malu did not open his eyes, even a wink.

Frustrated, she got to her feet. What else could she do? Maybe a strong aroma might do the trick. Some food, perhaps? She walked through the silent palace again and found the kitchen. What could she cook in a hurry? *Khichri* was the only dish she could think of. Where were the rice, the dal, the spices and the ghee? Rajula opened up container after container and managed to find all the ingredients. She rustled up a delicious *khichri*, fragrant with ghee, seasoned with the most aromatic spices—cinnamon, bay leaves, cloves and nutmeg. She served it on two *thalis*, carried it back steaming hot and placed it under his nose.

Malushahi's shapely nose twitched, he stirred again, muttered, then turned on his side and slept on.

Rajula could have wept! Why was the charm so potent? Why didn't Ija teach her a special mantra to remove its effect from her beloved, the way she had made Rajula safe from it?

What was she to do? She knew she could not linger. Her aim had been to come and tell Malu that she still loved him, and that if he loved her, too, he would have to come to her father's house and take her back as his bride. And if he didn't come soon, she would be transported across the mountains to Tibet and he would lose her forever. She had no choice but to leave a letter for him.

The *khichri* was too good to be wasted, so she ate her share first. Then she found a piece of *bhojpatra*—the birch bark they used to write upon, but there was no quill to write with.

A thought struck her—there was one way, which would be most effective. She felt under his pillow for the jewelled dagger she knew he always placed there at night. Gritting her teeth, she slit her finger. Then she removed her nose ring, dipped it in her blood and wrote a letter on the piece of *bhojpatra*:

My beloved Malushahi,
I came here to meet you, braving all kinds of peril. If you love me sincerely, and are a true son of your mother, you will come to my father's house and carry me back with honour as your bride. Only . . . I fear my father might harm you. Be careful, disguise yourself as a sadhu and bring your army along for your protection. But do not delay, else he'll send me across the mountains to Tibet and we will never meet again.

Yours and only yours,
Rajula

Rajula pinned the letter to a cushion with the dagger and crept out. Barely had she walked out of the gates when the palace began to stir.

By then Rajula was hurrying through the streets of the still slumbering town. The main part of her mission had been accomplished. The thought that she had not been able to talk to Malushahi lanced her heart painfully. But she had to return home as soon as she could. If by chance her father got back before her, it would be the end of all her planning. As she contemplated the journey back, she knew it would be foolhardy to risk all the dangers again. Now that she had proved her love for Malushahi, there was no reason to invite more trouble.

She drew a deep breath and chanted the spell to transform herself into a dove. Swiftly, she winged her way home.

13

A Painful Discovery

Malushahi sat up with a start. He was puzzled to find two *thalis* of food near his bed, one full, and the other empty. He was even more startled when his eye fell on the bloodstained dagger on his pillow. 'What's this?' He exclaimed, pulling it out and examining the letter. 'Who put this here?'

His eyes flew over the words. When he realized that he had slept through Rajula's visit, he cried out aloud. The letter fell from his hands as he jumped up and flung his pillow to the ground in frustration and stamped on it.

His voice rang though the corridors, alarming the maids. They rushed to inform the queen mother that her son was in distress and she hurried to his chamber at once.

'Oh, my son, my Malu! What ails you? Have you suddenly taken ill? Do you have an ache somewhere? Tell me and I'll send for the *vaidya* right away!

'No, no! It's nothing like that, Ija!' Malushahi cried, smiting his forehead with his clenched fist. 'My beloved Rajula came here and left, Ija, and like a fool, I slept the sleep of the dead! I, who have spent so many sleepless nights longing to meet her again ever since she vanished so mysteriously, slept like a dead man! I have to find her! If I can't, I'll renounce my wealth and my kingdom and become a sadhu. Call my commander-in-chief! I must set off for Jalnar Desh, the land of the Shaukas, and bring Rajula back as my wife.'

Dharma Devi paled. 'What were the guards doing? How did she enter the palace unnoticed?' Her voice turned hoarse with alarm as she clutched Malushahi's arm. 'I'm sure she used magic. I beg you to forget her, son, there are many beautiful maidens, much lovelier than her, right here in our kingdom. I can line up a hundred for you to choose from. Forget her! Do not venture into that land of mystery and magic.'

'I can't think of any other girl! I cannot even dream of marrying anyone else! If she used magic, it was because she had no choice. She is not a sorceress!' Malushahi banged his fist on the table nearby, making his mother jump. 'Don't try to dissuade me, Ija.'

'All right,' Dharma Devi hurriedly changed tack, 'but she couldn't have gone back so soon. Maybe she is still somewhere in the city. You don't have to go all that way to fetch her. Let us find out.'

Immediately, she summoned an old woman who was a skilled diviner. The diviner poured water into a new silver platter, peered into it. After a while she said, 'I see a dove flying northwards.'

The queen mother paled further. 'The Shaukas are well versed in magic, my son,' she clutched Malushahi's hands. 'You know . . . there are many kinds of sorcery—magic can cause terrible harm as well as help people. Why did she come here all alone? And why did she run away? Why did she not wait for you? Why didn't her father approach me to offer her hand in marriage? You are putting yourself at great risk, Malu. This could be a trap. Forget her for my sake, for your own, please, for the sake of this kingdom that is your responsibility.'

A deep frown furrowed Malushahi's broad forehead. He set his mouth stubbornly. 'Don't say that again, Ija. I cannot forget Rajula! She had to use magic to be able to reach me safely. Just think of the chances she took! All because she loves me so much. I have to follow her and bring her back as my bride.'

His mother stared at him, stunned. Then she quickly collected herself. 'All right . . . go if you insist . . . but will you give me a little time?' she coaxed. 'There's no need to rush headlong into danger. If you have to go, we need to think of a plan that is foolproof.'

Malushahi bit his lip, then nodded slowly. 'Make your plans, Ija,' he said, 'but I will not wait more than three days. Even that is too much. For Rajula to have come all this way, it means there's a grave threat.'

'Yes, yes,' his mother said eagerly. 'In three days everything will be in place. Rest assured, my son. Your happiness is my greatest concern.'

14

The False Rajula

Dharma Devi patted her son's shoulder and left for her chambers. Her mind was awhirl, wondering how to rid her son of this obsession. She summoned her most trusted maid Debuli immediately.

'A great calamity has befallen us, Debuli,' she whispered. 'Malu has fallen in love with a Shauka girl and insists on marrying her. We cannot let that happen.'

Debuli bowed low. 'We have to distract him somehow, your majesty. We need to replace her with another charming maiden.'

'Go and search the city!' the queen mother commanded. 'I don't care how you do it, but you must find the most beautiful, the most captivating girl in Bairath and bring her to the palace. If she is able to drive Rajula from the prince's heart, I will make her his queen. And you will be well rewarded.'

The shrewd maid smiled and bowed. Then she hurried out of the palace.

When a morose Malushahi sat down for his morning meal, after much coaxing, he was startled to find a strange girl serving him instead of the usual maid. She was dressed in a pink silk *ghaghra* that heightened the colour in her lovely face, necklaces of gold and coral reflected their gleam in her large lustrous eyes, and the scent of musk that wafted from her almost turned him dizzy.

'Who are you, *behni*?' he frowned as she ladled steaming *halwa* into his silver bowl. 'Since when have you begun to work in the palace?'

'My . . . my name is Rajula,' the girl replied in a faltering voice as the queen mother had instructed her.

'Rajula? You're lying. You cannot be Rajula! There is only one Rajula in the world and I would never address her as "sister!" Leave this place at once.' Sparks of rage flew from Malushahi's eyes.

The terrified girl dropped the dish she was holding and stepped back hastily.

Dharma Devi clucked her tongue loudly. 'Son, son,' she said. 'She is no less than the Shauka girl in beauty. Take a proper look at her, at least.'

Malushahi, however, pushed his food away and rose.

'No, Ija! I have discussed it all with you,' he said. 'I will not budge from my stand, no matter what you try. And . . .' he looked directly at his mother. 'I . . . I don't feel like attending the court today either, Ija. Will you take my place? My heart is so heavy and my mind in such turmoil that I'm bound to make wrong decisions. I . . . I don't want that to happen.'

Dharma Devi watched him stomp off, full of dismay. Then she collected herself enough to mutter to a maid, 'Follow him! Don't let him out of your sight for a minute!'

15
Malushahi's Flute

The maid ran after Malushahi, halting only to pick up a shawl to drape around her head and face. She followed the king as he listlessly stumbled towards the forest nearby. 'Why were you so impatient, Rajula,' he was muttering. 'Couldn't you have waited a few more moments? No . . . I wrong you! You took the greatest of risks coming all the way, all alone. I am the one at fault.' He let out a huge sigh, so full of grief that the maid couldn't help feeling tearful herself.

As she furtively wiped her eyes, she noticed that he had stopped in front of a bamboo grove, near a very tall bamboo plant. 'Baans Dajyu, my dear old friend,' Malushahi whispered. 'You have made so many flutes for me, those that played merry tunes, stirring martial ones, or those that simply mesmerized the listener. Today I'm looking for a different kind–my heart is so full of sorrow that I want a flute that only plays sad tunes.'

The maid started. Malushahi was known as a flute player whose music had a peculiar power over the listener. She could never have dreamt that he got his flutes from this bamboo grove. To her astonishment the tall bamboo rustled as if in response. She was even more flabbergasted when something came flying through the air and fell on the ground at the prince's feet. A flute!

She suppressed a gasp as Malushahi folded his hands gratefully, bowed low and picked up the flute. He found a large rock nearby and sat down on it. For a while he just sat there with the flute in his hands. Then he drew a deep breath and put it to his lips.

The tune that emerged brought a shiver of goose bumps to the maid's skin. Tears followed. The music was so overwhelmingly sad that they simply gushed down her cheeks. She didn't wait any longer. She dashed back to the palace helter-skelter to inform the queen mother.

By the time she reached, however, the sad strains of that flute were already spreading through the city. People paused in the midst of their work to wipe their tears, not knowing what was afflicting them. Carpenters halted their hammering, merchants were interrupted while counting their money, and housewives let their pots of rice scorch as they started to weep without knowing why. Some folk were so overcome that they simply abandoned whatever they were doing and sat immobile, sunk in gloom.

Dharma Devi, too, found herself sobbing uncontrollably for no apparent reason, while the bewildered courtiers struggled with an unexpected onslaught of grief. The cooks in the palace kitchen dropped their ladles and pots and pans, the guards shed tears as they patrolled, and large drops poured from the magnificent elephant's eyes. And when the guard dogs raised their heads and began to howl, it became unbearable.

Just then the maid rushed in crying, 'It's the flute, the sad flute. The king is playing the sad flute.'

Dharma Devi gazed at her astounded. 'What are you talking about?' she demanded.

'It's true, your majesty,' the maid whispered, bowing low. 'The king . . . our Malushahi . . . has acquired a flute that plays only sad tunes, from the bamboo grove in the forest . . . Its music brings on an unbearable melancholy.'

The queen mother smote her forehead and shook her head, preplexed.

'Do something, your majesty,' the courtiers flung themselves at her feet. 'Stop the king from playing that flute. We'll all die of misery. Bairath will be destroyed.'

Just then Malushahi entered the palace. As the tortured notes of the flute pierced everyone's ears, a loud wail resounded through the court.

Ghaghra skirts flying, Dharma Devi hurried to her son. 'My Malu,' she cried, clutching his arm, 'You can go to Jalnar Desh to bring your Rajula. Just stop playing that sad flute.'

Malushahi paused and stared at her, then a smile spread over his face. 'Oh Ija, you're the best mother that ever was.' The sad flute dropped from his hands as he bent to embrace his mother. One of the courtiers quickly spirited it away and hid it.

'But we have to make proper plans, son,' Dharma Devi's face was taut with anxiety. 'I must consult the gurus—Khekidas and Bekhidas—the teachers who advise you on everything. But let me visit them first and explain everything.'

'Of course, Ija! You know how much I revere our gurus. How can we move without their advice?'

Dharma Devi sent for her palanquin and made her way to the gurus' abode.

'Venerable gurus, I beg you to help me,' she cried. 'Raja Malushahi is madly in love with Rajula, a girl from the Jalnar Desh. If he cannot marry her, he says, he'll become an ascetic. He insists on going to that dreaded land to fetch her. You know he's my only child, born with such difficulty. I fear most grievously for his life. Please, I beseech you to accompany him on the journey to that fearful place. Protect him with your great knowledge.'

The gurus, father and son, looked at each other. 'I can understand your great anxiety,' Khekidas said. 'But do not worry. I will go with him and see that he comes to no harm.'

16

An Army on the March

Dharma Devi hurried back to tell Malushahi what the guru had said. Full of excitement at the thought that he would soon bring Rajula back to be his bride, he rushed to the guru's dwelling.

The moment he entered, Malushahi prostrated himself at the guru's feet. His eyes were bright with unshed tears as he said, 'You have saved my life, venerable Gurujyu. The truth is, I cannot live unless I marry Rajula. Please accept my deepest gratitude for agreeing to accompany me to Jalnar Desh.'

Khekidas placed his hand on Malushahi's head. His face was serious as he replied, 'It is an extremely dangerous undertaking, my son. But if we are well prepared, there is nothing to fear. We must go disguised as sadhus and I will arm myself with all the magic powers I possess. First, we must collect all the able-bodied men in the kingdom to accompany us on our mission. If it comes to a battle, we will need a strong army. Please sound the magic drum to summon them.'

Malushahi sprang up immediately. A huge drum hung in front of the guru's house. It was said to possess magical properties but could only be sounded when the guru ordered it. Malushahi seized the drumstick that was as long as a young pine tree and swung at the drum with all the strength his muscular arms possessed.

A deafening sound emerged, a sound so loud that it reverberated through his whole kingdom, reached even the remotest corners. And everywhere, the moment that hollow boom knocked at their eardrums, men abandoned whatever they were doing.

Farmers paused while tilling their fields to exclaim, 'Did you hear that? It's the magic drum! The king needs us, we must hurry to Bairath.'

Herders quickly drove their cattle home, shouting, 'The royal summons has come. We must go to the palace immediately.'

Shopkeepers, goldsmiths and blacksmiths, carpenters and masons—all the strong young men in Katyur stopped working and headed for the capital. Soon crowds of volunteers clustered around the guru's house.

Malushahi's breath quickened when he set eyes on them.

Once almost all the physically fit men in Katyur had assembled, he addressed them: 'My brave men,' he said, 'I need you to accompany me on a dangerous journey. Are you willing?'

The cry that went up was almost as loud as the booming of the magic drum. 'Yes, yes, Maharaj! We will follow you unto death itself!'

Malushahi took a deep breath and continued: 'I am touched by your love and loyalty. But for the success of this difficult quest we have to go in disguise. We will don the garb of ascetics. And since we cannot waste even a minute, we must begin to get ready right away.'

Barely had he finished speaking when the men got on the job. They went from house to house asking women to donate iron *karahis*. Hundreds were collected. The blacksmiths got busy at once, melting them down to fashion the tongs sadhus always carried. Brass pots were transformed into *kundals* to dangle in the ascetics' ears and *kamandals* for the alms they would receive. Each household in the city contributed ash, too, from its kitchen fire, and the young men threw off their clothes and rubbed it on their faces, their arms and legs, and all over their bare bodies. Then they donned saffron robes and proclaimed they were ready for the mission.

It was an impressive band that set off, shouting the invocation, '*Bam-bam Bhole!*' The earth quaked under their feet and the sky turned so dark with the dust they stirred that people in distant villages cowered, wondering what calamity was approaching. When they got closer, however, young men rushed to the ranks of the ascetic-soldiers, spurred by the idea of the mission.

After marching for several days, they reached a pleasant spot that lay between two hills.

'Shall we set up camp here tonight?' Malushahi asked.

'This is Homdhura,' Guru Khekidas said. 'We are not too far from our destination. But, what is the matter, Maharaj? Are you all right?'

'I . . . I don't know. I'm feeling a little dizzy.' Malushahi put a hand to his head, then muttered, 'Oh, look! That man has fainted. Th-that one t-too!' He was swaying on his feet, his speech was beginning to slur as well. He reached out to grasp the branch of a tree, then sat down heavily on a nearby rock.

'What's happening?' 'H-help!' Men were crying out all around them, staggering, slumping to the ground like felled trees.

'This place is bewitched!' the guru exclaimed. 'But I have come prepared. I armed myself with fifty-two magic spells before leaving.'

Immediately he produced a pouch from his bag, sprinkled handfuls of the powder inside it in the air and began to chant a mantra, circling round the prostrate forms.

Slowly, the unconscious ascetic-soldiers began to sit up, rub their eyes and get to their feet.

'You saved us, Gurujyu!' Malushahi prostrated himself at Khekidas's feet. The men followed suit. 'If you hadn't come with us, we would never have been able to reach Rajula. But how did this happen? I didn't notice anyone around!'

'Your honourable mother was justified in her fears. The very air in this place is poisonous. We will be more cautious now.'

After spending the night there, the band of ascetics crossed the Hyunli Ganga River and arrived at Kankarikhal, which was very close to Rajula's village.

'All seems well, here, Gurujyu.' Malushahi took a deep breath. His face was flushed with excitement. The men were busy pitching tents and cooking fires had started to flicker amidst them. 'I can't wait to go and find Rajula!'

'We need to send a couple of scouts to make sure first, my son,' the guru cautioned. 'Who knows what dangers are waiting to ambush us? I'll find a way to inform Rajula that you've arrived.'

Guru Khekidas summoned a few men. 'It is time to begin the task we came here for. Go into the village and ask for alms. Don't eat any food they offer you,' he warned them, 'nor drink any water. Just accept what they give you and return. If any of you come across Rajula, try to inform her secretly that Malushahi is here.'

17

Hope Revived

Rajula returned home from Bairath just in time. The very next afternoon after she got back, the hoof beats of her father's horses resounded in her ears. She shivered as she caught sight of them, wondering what the outcome might have been had she taken the same route back, and thanked heaven for her mother's magic spells.

'Everything has been settled,' she heard her father tell her mother. 'In a week's time, Rikhyepal will arrive. Your daughter will be married, Ganguli! Aren't you overjoyed that she'll be a queen?'

'Yes, yes, of course, I am!' Rajula could imagine her mother hurriedly forcing her mouth into a smile, concealing the alarm her daughter's keen ear had caught in her voice. 'Which mother wouldn't be overjoyed at such good fortune for her daughter? My only concern is . . . that she'll be so far away. Who knows when I'll get to see her, once she's gone?' Ganguli gulped down a sob.

'I will miss her, too,' Sunapati sounded grave, 'but you know well that daughters are born to leave their parents' homes. We must not be selfish; we must pray for her happiness and prosperity. Rikhyepal himself asked for her hand. She will tread on roses there and sleep on a bed lined with silk and satin.'

Listening, Rajula suppressed a sigh. Her father talked of praying for her happiness, but was he really concerned enough to marry her to a man who would make her truly happy? The thought that the Tibetan king would arrive in a week's time made her shudder with dread. What was Malushahi doing right now? Had he seen her message and how would he respond? Did he care enough to come and take her away as his bride, before the Tibetan ruler came? And how would he manage that? Fear clawed at her heart.

A couple of days passed—excruciating days for Rajula, days when she could hardly sit still, her nerves on edge and her heart fluttering like a butterfly being chased.

'Do not lose heart, my child,' her mother said, drawing her close, as she came upon Rajula hunched up in a corner, weeping. She stroked her back with a gentle hand. 'There is still time.'

'I wonder, Ija.' Rajula bit her trembling lip.

Her eyes had been scanning the horizon constantly, hoping to catch a glimpse of strange men approaching the village, Malushahi leading them. She had no inkling what course he might pursue to rescue her; all she could do was to pray that he was on his way.

Two days passed thus after her father's arrival, two tortured days. And then on the third she heard a call, 'Alms, my good people, alms for a poor sadhu!'

Her heart executed a gigantic leap. Could it be him? She had suggested he disguise himself as a sadhu. Fortunately, her father was not at home. She ran to her mother.

'Ija, there's a sadhu outside. Can I give him some rice?'

'Of course,' her mother replied. She hurried to the store room and scooped out a large bowl of uncooked rice from an earthen jar. 'Give this to the holy man,' she said, then whispered under her breath, 'and ask him where he's from.'

Rajula could not help smiling. The same thoughts were passing through her mother's mind.

Disappointment clouded her face when she saw that it was not Malushahi standing there. 'Heaven bless you, daughter,' the bearded man proclaimed in a hoarse voice. 'May all your wishes be fulfilled. I am on the brink of starvation–it's a long way here, from Bairath.' The last words were spoken in an undertone and she was thankful they were. Because just as she was stepping back, a shadow darkened the ground. Rajula suppressed a start.

Her father was back!

'Well done, my child,' he said. 'We must always give whatever we can to holy men. He will pray for a happy married life for you, that you be blessed with many children. Won't you, Sadhu Baba? This girl is to be married in a few days' time.'

'Of course, I will,' the ascetic replied. 'May heaven shower all its blessings upon you, my daughter.'

Rajula folded her hands and bowed.

The sadhu was just turning away when Sunapati asked, 'Do you belong to the group of mendicants camping at Kankarikhal?'

The man nodded. 'Indeed I do.'

Sunapati smiled. 'Please carry a message to your leader. I, Sunapati Shauka, would like to invite the venerable sadhus for a meal tonight.'

The sadhu paused for a moment before replying. He raised a hand in blessing as he spoke, 'May you live a thousand years, generous one! I will convey your message to our guru.'

Rajula stood there, overcome with a peculiar unease. The thought that Malushahi might be among the group turned her giddy with delight. At the same time a horrible fear crawled down her back. Suppose her father recognized him when he came?

There was no time or opportunity to discuss anything with her mother. The moment Baujyu entered the house he began to call out, 'Ganguli! Ganguli, I have invited a group of sadhus to eat with us tonight. There are many of them. I want you to prepare a feast they will not forget in a hurry, because I seek their blessings for a happy future for our Rajula.'

Something about the way he said this—with an underlying threat lacing every word—made Rajula apprehensive. Somehow she forced herself to calm her fears. Soon she was drawn into such a flurry of preparations with her mother and her helpers that she forgot it all.

Only when the goat's-milk *kheer* that was being prepared for dessert was simmering on the wood fire did her misgivings resurface—because her father appeared. This was unusual. He normally did not enter the kitchen, where the women prepared the food. He hovered in between the women kneading dough for puris, peered into the large *karahi*. 'Are you sure it's sweet enough?' he demanded. 'Ganguli, your *kheer* is always short of sweetening. Let me add some of this special honey. You know the honey gathered in the month of Kartik is most beneficial!'

Rajula glanced up in surprise. This was a rare occurrence—her father taking so much interest in the cooking. A helper was holding a jar of honey saved from the previous year. Sunapati poured a generous amount into the *kheer*. 'I hope there are enough almonds in it, too!' he continued.

'I put them myself,' her mother replied, somewhat irritably.

Rajula was relieved when he went away; she was not sure why.

The call *'Bam-bam Bhole!'* signalled the arrival of the sadhus.

Sunapati ushered them into the stone-paved courtyard, bowing at their feet, saying, 'What an honour to host so many holy men! A poor man like me rarely has the opportunity.' Rajula scanned their faces anxiously as he seated them in rows on the deerskin he had specially arranged for. Which one was her Malu? Her eyes flickered over their faces. It was hard to identify anyone under the coating of ash, the unkempt beards and the tangled locks of hair. But how could she miss him? His well-knit frame, the slight swagger with which he made his way to his seat—that could not be disguised! She hid her smile beneath her hand, concealed the flash of delight under her lowered lashes, as she began to serve the sumptuous meal that had been prepared for the sadhus on the leaf plates laid out before them. Her father must not get the slightest inkling of whom he was entertaining so lavishly.

She kept her face demure and expressionless as she ladled an extra-large helping of *alu gutak*—potatoes fragrant with turmeric and garlic, followed it with yams simmered in a creamy gravy, bright orange pumpkin, tender green mustard leaves redolent with garlic and chillies, the finest yoghurt, and hot, crisp puris.

The sadhus were feasting heartily, asking for second helpings and Sunapati Shauka beamed with delight as he watched them.

'Be ready tonight,' Malushahi whispered, as she bent over to place yet another puri in his leaf plate. 'Wait for the owl's hoot.'

Rajula didn't dare reply, just blinked rapidly to show that she'd heard.

'Ah, it's been a long time since we feasted on such delicious fare,' Malushahi went on in a loud voice, turning to address one of his companions.

Rajula managed a weak smile though her heart was a-flutter. She repeated a silent prayer of gratitude. At last fortune was smiling upon her!

'Ganguli, have you served the *kheer*?' she heard her father say. His tone was so gentle, and such a benign smile curved his mouth as he gestured, that Rajula experienced an unexpected spasm of guilt. If only he knew on whom he was raining this hospitality!

The moon was already burnishing the snow-covered Himalayas with a silvery sheen when the holy men left. Their blessings for their host and his family resounded in the silence that lay over the village, interrupted only by gentle music of the Goriganga River.

'If there's anything more I can do to make you comfortable, just say the word, venerable Gurujyu,' Sunapati said to Guru Khekidas with folded hands as he bade them goodbye. 'It is my privilege to serve you. I feel particularly fortunate that you have favoured us with your presence just before my daughter's wedding.'

He stood there, watching them make their way down the winding path. Soon his expression changed.

As they walked down the path, the sadhus' feet suddenly became unsteady. They lurched this way and that like men who had drunk too much. Sunapati followed them at a distance. They were not even halfway to Kankarikhal when one by one they began to keel over and fall to the ground. Malushahi was the last to be affected. He gazed at the others, turning breathless with anxiety as an awful fear became visible on his face. A crooked smile curved Sunapati's thin lips as he observed Malushahi staring at his companions and battling the dizziness that was overtaking him. Soon the king, too, lay sprawled on the ground.

The moment the troop of sadhus all lay spread out like lifeless bundles of clothes, Sunapati called out to his servants.

'Hurry up and finish the job,' he said. They came running to the scene. One by one they carried the Katyuris off and threw them into the icy caves that lay north of the village.

When they had all been disposed of, Sunapati surveyed the scene with satisfaction. 'That was a sumptuous feast, wasn't it? But the *kheer* was too much for you, my dear Malushahi. Too much for your dear friends, too. You thought you could fool me, Sunapati Shauka? Thought you could steal my daughter away from under my nose, instead of asking for her hand like an honourable man? Now you can lie here unconscious for the next one month. My magic potion will guarantee that. And if the bears do not get to you, the cold is likely to freeze you to death. By then Rajula will be far beyond your reach. Ha!'

Rajula lay on her bed, tossing and turning. She had not changed into her nightclothes. Surreptitiously she had tied up a couple of changes in a bundle. When would she hear the owl's call? Each distant sound made her start up eagerly. But the night trickled away like water leaking from a cracked pot and there was not the faintest hint of an owl's hoot to be heard.

The stars doused their lights, one by one. The sky began to lighten. With an enormous effort Rajula swallowed the huge wail that was rising to her throat. It roiled and moiled in her stomach like a captive beast. But she forced her rampaging thoughts, her stormy emotions, to be still. Weeping would not help; she had to try and think clearly. What could have happened? Had Malushahi taken ill? Or . . . the thought made her heart plummet, had he changed his mind? Whatever it was, she had to find out.

The moment dawn broke, she wrapped a large shawl around her head and crept to the door. Maybe she could get to Kankarikhal and find out why Malu had not stuck to his plans.

As soon as she unlatched the door, however, a heavy footstep resounded behind her. Her father.

'Where are you off to, my dear child?'

'Nowhere, Baujyu. I just wanted some fresh air. Ate too much last night.'

'So did our guests. It seems that our food filled the holy men with so much energy that I hear they've flown back over the mountains, back to the place they had come from.' He smiled and something in the way he looked at her brought a creeping terror. It tightened itself around Rajula's heart like a band of ice.

Something had happened to Malushahi—something horrifying, and her father was responsible.

She turned, ignoring his comment. 'I thought you wanted to get some fresh air.' There was a confident smirk in his voice.

Her legs were as shaky as a newborn lamb's as she tottered back into her room. Suddenly, all her resolution fled. She let her wails echo through the house as she abandoned herself to despair.

All her mother's comforting and coaxing brought no relief. She gave up eating and was preparing to starve herself to death till her mother said, 'What will you gain by giving up your life, child? You tried your best to reunite with Malushahi, but fate willed otherwise. You are young; there is so much to look forward to. And have you ever thought of your mother? How will I live if you insist on this course?'

Rajula's tears flowed again when Ganguli said this. An uncontrollable feeling of rebellion seized her again. Why did only her father's will prevail? His and only his? Why couldn't her wishes be taken into account? She would abandon her fast, if only it was to find a way to defy her father. And . . . maybe Malu was still alive somewhere. How could she believe that someone so strong could be snuffed out just like that?

'I'll drink some milk, Ija,' she said.

Three days passed. Seventy-two hours of feverish, whirling thought. Just one thought. How could she be reunited with Malu again? She refused to believe that he was dead.

18

The Wedding

All around, preparations for Rajula's wedding were afoot. Cooks sat before huge fires outside, stirring *khoya* for sweets, frying golden *badas* and various other savouries, filling the air with appetizing aromas. The musicians beat on their *dhols* from morning till late at night, the *turi* and *ransingha* joined in with their shrill wail, while the women's songs of celebration added their clamour. These sounds brought no joy, no sense of festivity to Rajula; to her they carried the despair of a mourner's funereal cries.

A few days later the news she had been dreading arrived.

'Rikhyepal has sent a messenger,' her father's voice rang jubilantly through the house. 'He will be here tomorrow. Hurry, Ganguli! All the arrangements must be complete by tonight.'

'Why are you getting so anxious?' Ganguli retorted shrilly. 'Her clothes are ready, the cooks have been working for days. All the material for the ceremony has been put together. Today we finished painting the auspicious *aipan* patterns on the floors. All we need to do is to put up the ceremonial gate and prepare the wedding *mandap*. Get your men to cut down some banana trees and fetch flowers for it!'

Crouched in her room, Rajula started up. She had not wanted to believe that the wedding would actually happen, despite all the preparatory activity. She was sure that a miracle, some divine intervention would reunite her with Malu. One morning she would wake up and find that this was just a bad dream.

Her father's words hit her like a death sentence. They drove her into an unbearable panic. A hollow opened up in her belly, forcing her to acknowledge that she could not wait any longer. She had to make a last attempt to escape her fate.

What could she do? How could she get away, find Malu again? Her mother's charms! How could she have forgotten them? They were hidden right here in her room. With trembling hands she tore out the bag she had stored them in, riffled through the contents frantically. Which spell would work best? The amulet? She pulled it out and repeated the mantra in a quavering voice. Would it work?

It did. Within seconds she was zooming over the valleys in the form of a dove, searching desperately. She flew up and down, over hill and vale, but found nothing, not a shred of cloth, nor even the cold ashes of a cooking fire . . . It was as if Malushahi and his men had never come here and it had all been a dream.

She had barely returned home and turned back to her human form when her mother entered the room.

'Ija!' Rajula cried, clutching her shoulders. 'You . . . you know I can't marry the Tibetan king. Do something, please!'

Her mother dropped her eyes. 'It's no use now, my child, it's too late,' she said in a dead voice. 'You . . . I . . . we both tried whatever we could . . . now you must accept your fate. Your bridegroom has arrived. You have to start getting ready for the wedding ceremonies.'

Rajula sat down heavily on her bed. She was too numb to weep.

'Come on, my child,' her mother stroked her hair. 'Everything will be fine.'

An overpowering rage flared within Rajula. She couldn't abandon herself to her destiny. Despite the ominous thoughts that plagued her, the chilling visions of Malu lying cold and dead, it was impossible to accept that she had no choice.

Now as she clutched her head desperately as if to squeeze some remedy out, her only thought was, was there any way she could turn all this to her advantage? She drew a deep breath as an idea shuddered up from her belly, a thought as soothing as a warm cup of milk and honey clutched in cold hands on a chilly evening.

She turned to her mother. 'Maybe you are right, Ija. I tried to fight my fate, but my most determined efforts did not accomplish anything.' She was careful to keep her voice as broken as she could because she knew dissemblance was her best weapon now. 'I will get ready, I promise, but before the ceremony, please send the pandit who will perform it to me. There are some questions I would like to ask him. But in secret.'

Ganguli's brow furrowed. Her eyes bored suspiciously into Rajula. Rajula's heart thumped. Had her mother guessed? She knew her too well, knew how intractable she was and how hard it was for her to give up. Then she glanced away as if she preferred not to know. 'As you wish, my child,' she said expressionlessly. 'But I'm sending the girls to help you dress in your bridal attire. The auspicious hour is approaching. You don't wish to invite further bad luck, I hope.'

'Don't worry, Ija. I'll be ready in a trice.' Rajula's mouth trembled into a smile.

Ganguli beckoned one of the maids to help Rajula put on her gold-embroidered velvet *ghaghra* and went off to search for the pandit. She found him at the *mandap*, almost hidden behind the banana fronds, busy arranging all the material he needed for the wedding ceremony—the coconuts, turmeric and vermilion, the rice, the silver vessels, the *paan* and *supari* and the sprigs of sacred *doob* grass.

'Panditji,' she said, 'my daughter has a last-minute request before the ceremony begins. She wants to ask you something. Can you spare a moment for her?'

The man stared at her uncomprehendingly for a moment, then he nodded, though perplexity still ruffled his brow. 'Indeed, I can.'

Ganguli accompanied him to Rajula's room. She was ready now. A heavy gold necklace was clasped around her throat and a large gem-studded nose ring glittered on her cheek. But she looked deathly pale, despite the sheen of her bright pink head covering.

Ganguli sucked in her breath. Her hands reached towards her daughter, then fell.

Rajula did not seem to notice. 'This is for your ears alone, Panditjyu,' she said, her voice cold and expressionless.

'In any case, I need to go and attend to something,' Ganguli said, flushing. 'Come with me,' she beckoned to the maid.

'What is it, my child?' asked the pandit, keeping his eyes correctly downcast. 'Is it some point of religion, some question about the ceremony?'

In reply Rajula pulled a ring from her finger. A large gleaming sapphire set in gold, it looked fabulously expensive. She held it out on her palm.

'I wanted to give you a gift,' Rajula said. 'Do you like this ring?'

The pandit shrank back as if it were a snake she was offering. His shrivelled mouth fell open and his bony shoulders jerked. Forgetting all decorum, he looked Rajula in the eye as if trying to find an explanation for her odd behaviour.

'What are you saying, my child? It's your father's duty to reward me, not yours! What will he say if he hears of this?' The pandit's voice quavered. 'Why do you want to do this?'

Rajula twisted the end of her veil around a slender finger. 'My father does not need to know,' she murmured.

The pandit choked on another gasp.

Now Rajula looked him squarely in the eye. 'I want you to take it . . . All I ask is a small favour in return.'

'No-no!'

'You have to do it!' Rajula's voice was as menacing as her father's could be and the priest trembled. 'Tell them that the hour is not auspicious. Tell them that the wedding can be performed in Tibet, too—at the right time.'

The priest glanced at the ring, then knotted his gnarled fingers together and twisted them round and round. 'I-I can't do it! But . . . but why, my child? What difference will it make?'

'I have my reasons. Just do as I say and . . . this ring will be yours.'

Rajula held up the ring and twirled it round and round—slowly. It flashed a potent blue fire, dazzling the priest. The man knew this was a very lucky stone. He was the one who had suggested Sunapati buy it for his daughter to stave off misfortune and confer prosperity on her. 'You can hide it. My father will never find out . . .' Rajula whispered. 'Didn't you say the stone had powerful qualities, apart from its great value?

Finally, greed got the better of the pandit. 'All right,' he said.

With trembling hands, he reached out for the ring.

'What are you saying? The time is not auspicious? But you yourself suggested it. You had worked it all out!' The bridegroom cried out. His dismay was almost comical as he lifted up the gold chains that fell over his face, suspended from the jewelled tiara framing his forehead.

'Please forgive me . . .' the priest folded his hands and bowed. 'I . . . I was doing a last-minute check and realized I had made a mistake in my calculations. I . . . I don't want any misfortune to befall our dear daughter—and . . . and her future husband.' The pandit's voice was as smooth as butter.

Sunapati's brow turned as black as a moonless night. He stamped his foot so hard that the pandit shrank away. 'If . . . if it is acceptable to our honourable Sunapatijyu, it can be performed in your country at the appropriate time, Maharaj. If he agrees that you can take your bride back with you, with suitable companions as chaperones.'

Sunapati's eyes bored into the pandit's face. Then his shoulders slumped. 'I . . . I certainly don't want my daughter married at an inauspicious moment. But it will not be easy for you to come again. Let me think . . .'

He turned his back and paced up and down for several minutes. Then he halted and flung a stern glance at the priest. 'The pandit will accompany you and solemnize the marriage when he has studied his astrological charts properly. Get ready for the journey, Panditjyu!'

'Of course, of course, Sunapatijyu!' The priest's frame trembled as he bowed.

The bridegroom shook his head and talked vehemently in his own language to his companions. Then he exhaled heavily, shrugged and nodded.

Sunapati himself went to inform his daughter. Rajula camouflaged her surge of joy with a bewildered frown, and exclaimed, 'But, Baujyu . . . how is this possible?'

'It is all right, my child, perfectly all right.'

Ganguli wept bitterly as Rajula stepped into the silver palanquin. Even Sunapati brushed a rough hand across his face. But Rajula displayed no emotion—just embraced her mother quietly and bowed to her father as he blessed her.

The auspicious songs faded behind her, the shrill sound of the horns stilled as the palanquin was carried up the steep slopes. She stared at the jagged outlines of the tall evergreens, the silvery tops of the mountains looming up before her and wondered what lay ahead. The guttural voice of her bridegroom grazed her ears over the yaks' irritable grunts, as he talked on incessantly to his companions. Not knowing his language, she wondered about what. Was he complaining? Was he annoyed? He had seemed to accept the priest's verdict.

She smiled, safe behind the curtain of her veil. She would be back, she thought with determination. Only . . . Malushahi would have to cross the mountains to fetch her. She had set him a real task this time and he would have to prove equal to it. Would he? He had answered her call, and . . . if all was well with him, she was sure he would. The journey might be far harder, but he would not have to confront her father this time.

19

The Rescue

Dharma Devi sat in her chambers, fingering her prayer beads. Several days had passed without any news of Malushahi, and she was wan with anxiety. Now she could not bear it any longer. She summoned the chief minister.

'Malu should have been back by now,' she said, biting her lip. 'Oh, why did he go? It was too dangerous an undertaking. I'm afraid, terrified . . . he might have fallen victim to some evil design. We must find out what has transpired, despatch a strong force in case he needs aid.'

'Maharaj possesses the strength and valour that befits a king, your majesty. It is also a long distance to travel and the terrain is very rugged. He might already be on his way back,' the chief minister replied.

'I know that . . . but I can't help feeling uneasy,' Dharma Devi shook her head. 'A-a few days back . . . I had an awful dream.' Her mouth twisted as she continued, 'I . . . I saw his corpse lying in a field of snow. I fear the worst. I can't wait any longer! Please send for my brother, Mrityunjaya Singh Garhwali, right away.'

The minister's face turned grave. 'I hope and pray your premonition turns out to be false, your majesty. But I will despatch a messenger right away.'

The messenger rode hard and fast, but still, a week went by before Mrityunjaya Singh arrived.

By this time Dharma Devi was convinced that some serious ill had befallen her son. She welcomed her brother eagerly.

'I told him not to go, I begged him!' she wept as she embraced him. 'I tried my best to stop him, but that enchantress had cast such a powerful spell on him that he wouldn't listen to me. How will we save him now? Oh, my beloved son, how can I get you back?' She paused and wiped her tears. 'The worst is that all the able-bodied men accompanied him. There are only a few guards and older men left. How can such a huge army vanish like that? It's unimaginable!'

'Don't lose heart so easily.' Her brother held up a comforting hand. 'If it is as you fear and he's fallen prey to some kind of sorcery, you well know that the most powerful magic spells can be countered. Call your best diviners and magicians, and instruct your remaining men to get ready at once.'

'I will,' Dharma Devi replied. She hesitated for a moment before continuing, 'There's one thing bothering me . . . Do you remember how I visited the temple of Chitrashila

Devi before he was born?' Her brother nodded. 'We met a couple there and I exchanged a vow with the woman—that we would get our children married to each other if one was a boy and one a girl . . . I can't help wondering if this girl is their child . . . they were from Jalnar Desh, too. I don't know why I forgot about that promise . . . and they didn't contact me either.'

Mrityunjaya sighed. 'It's too late to think of all this now. We are losing time and every small delay will work against us. Right now we have to save Malu somehow.'

Within hours, the rescue force, just a meagre fraction of the enormous army that had accompanied Malushahi, had been organized. Soon they were speeding over hill and vale. When they reached Kankarikhal, the place where Malushahi and his followers had camped and close to where they lay unconscious, one of the diviners exclaimed: 'Stop! I can sense Maharaj's spirit—somewhere close by.'

He pulled out his divining tools, flung rice and vermilion powder into the air as he repeated the incantation that located hidden objects:

'Earth or sky,
Fire or ice,
Close or far,
Deep or high,
I'll find you with
My all-seeing eye . . .'

Mrityunjaya watched anxiously as the man went into a trance. After a while, the diviner opened his eyes and spoke in the slurred monotonous voice of someone waking from a deep slumber.

'In a cave
Upon a hill,
Lies the king
Deathly still!'

'But which one?' asked the king's uncle, running his eyes over the rows of hills that surrounded them, stretching on and on.

Just then a raven squawked loudly.

'Oh, get rid of this inauspicious bird!' the diviner cried out, annoyed.

Some of the men tried to shoo the huge bird away, but it would not budge and continued to squawk insistently.

Mrityunjaya Singh's eyes narrowed. 'I think we have misunderstood. It is trying to tell us something,' he said. In a softer voice he continued, fixing his gaze on the raven, 'What is it, Kagaraj? What do you know? Can you help us?'

The raven flew down from the branch, hopped around in a circle and then flapped its wings. Then, as they watched, puzzled, it rose into the air.

'Follow it, at once!' Mrityunjaya cried out.

The soldiers clambered over the slopes, following the bird as it winged its way to a nearby hill, stopping to perch on a branch whenever the men fell behind.

And then one of the soldiers exclaimed: 'I can see some caves!'

The dark mouths of caves yawning on the hillside were clearly visible. Glistening patches of snow still lay around them. The men hurried up the slope in groups, eager to reach them.

As they approached the first one, an eager young soldier darted ahead and peered into it. 'There . . . there's a man . . . lying on the ground!' he cried out.

Mrityunjaya, who had halted to catch his breath, stepped forward quickly. 'Hmm . . . you're right . . .' His face turned grim as the outline of a human form became clear in the murky half-light.

It was large cave, much larger than they could have guessed from its opening.

'Here's another!' 'And another!'

One after the other, members of Malushahi's army became visible.

'Oh, here's Gurujyu . . . and . . . and here's the king . . .'

Malushahi lay there, his eyes closed, still as death. His body was icy cold to the touch when Mrityunjaya bent to examine it.

Tears streamed down an old soldier's eyes as he placed a hesitant hand on the king's feet. 'Look what they've done to our beloved Maharaj,' he wept.

Another man rushed forward and tried to rub life into Malushahi's frozen feet. After a while, he gave up, shaking his head. 'It's no use . . .' he said.

'We can't use ordinary means to revive the king and his soldiers.' Mrityunjaya Singh shook his head brusquely. 'Only magic can counter magic. I can see that a powerful spell has been used.' He turned to the sorcerers who had just arrived on the scene. 'This is the time for your to prove your skills. We *have* to bring them all back to life!'

The magicians immediately produced their charms and potions and set to work along with Mrityunjaya, who began to chant the death-defying mantra he was named after.

It took seven days and seven nights for the young king to return to life, along with Guru Khekidas and his men.

Malushahi sat up slowly, stretched and cast a baffled gaze all around. When his eyes fell on his uncle, he rose and touched his feet. 'When did you arrive, Mamjyu? And what am I doing here in this desolate place?' All of a sudden his face twisted. 'Rajula . . . I was to bring her back . . . What happened?'

'You fell victim to her father's magic, son,' his uncle said gently.

Malushahi struck his forehead. 'What a fool I've been! I should have been more cautious. What a fool!'

He fell silent and buried his face in his hands. His once strong frame, shrunk to skin and bone after his ordeal, slumped over in despair.

'What will I do if her father has married her off to Rikhyepal?'

Guru Khekidas cleared his throat. 'It was my fault, too. As your guru I should have anticipated it. I believed that the spells I used before we left for Sunapati's house would counter his magic . . . But do not abandon hope, my son. Let us try and find out at least what has happened to Rajula.'

'We need to plan even more carefully this time,' Mrityunjaya said. 'Who knows what other tricks Sunapati has in store? We need disguises that no one can see through.'

'Yes, we have to try and become part of the landscape so he doesn't notice anything out of the ordinary.' Khekidas tugged at his straggly beard.

'Maybe . . . we can fool him by assuming forms that are not human,' Mrityunjaya said.

'Indeed . . . that may be the only way,' Khekidas nodded seriously.

20

A Dismal Journey

The road wound up higher and higher as their journey progressed. Rajula had often travelled over the steep hills and lush valleys of her native Jalnar with her family, but she had never set eyes on such sheer heights, such threatening precipices.

Her gaze grew wide and apprehensive as the white walls of snow began to rise around her. A fit of shivering seized her suddenly, so overpowering that she could not control it despite all the woollen clothes she was wrapped in, even when she huddled inside the bearskin her mother had placed in the palanquin just as she was leaving.

'It will be bitterly cold on the way, child,' Ija had said, brushing away a tear. 'You will need this to protect yourself.'

All of a sudden, Rajula's heart began to plummet. Why had she agreed to go to Tibet? Why hadn't she run away and let her father do his worst? And . . . how would Malushahi ever negotiate these treacherous slopes when he came to rescue her? She had set him an impossible task. Hot tears scorched her numb cheeks as she thought of the dismal prospect that lay ahead. She would never see Malushahi again, nor her parents.

She had lost everyone she loved.

'We are crossing the passes–the most difficult part of our journey,' she heard someone say. 'Once we're through we will stop to rest. After this it will become much more comfortable.' It was Rikhyepal. Surprisingly, he was quite fluent in her language and seemed kindly. But that was small consolation.

Rajula nodded and wiped her tears, though the words did not provide any cheer. The barren, deserted landscape added to her sense of isolation. Not a single tree, nor even a tiny shrub to relieve its bleakness. Not a single human being to be seen apart from their own travelling party. Worse, an eerie silence lay like a grim curse over the mountains surrounding them on all sides like fortress walls. Soon, a fine, powdery snow began to descend on them, making her feel even more disoriented. Just then, an unexpected sound–the cheeping of a bird startled her.

'Can any creature survive this desolate place?' she asked.

Rikhyepal let out an expletive. 'It's that accursed snowbird,' he said. 'Only a creature like it can exist in these climes.'

'Accursed?' Rajula asked.

'Yes!' he replied abruptly. 'And don't ask me more. It's an ill-omened creature!'

Mystified, and a little apprehensive, Rajula could not help opening the curtain of her palanquin a tiny bit to take a look. A small white bird flew by. Her eyes almost popped out when its chirping began to take the shape of human speech. Was it . . . was it actually talking in a human voice?

'There is no hope for you, Rikhyepal!' The bird's voice had the harsh rhythm of hailstones falling on a slate roof. 'This girl can never be yours.'

A guttural sound tore out of Rikhyepal's throat. Horrified, Rajula watched him pull out his dagger and aim it at the bird. A futile gesture—because before he could do anything, it had merged into the snowy whiteness.

Rajula dropped the curtain at once. Her hand flew to her heart. It was pummelling the walls of her chest like a small insistent fist. Had the bird really spoken, or was she imagining it? But Rikhyepal had definitely drawn his dagger in response. A wild surge of hope warmed her through and through. Why would the bird say such a thing unless her fate lay elsewhere? Perhaps Malu would be able to make this perilous journey successfully. How she hoped it would happen! But she would have to do her bit, too—use all her wits and powers of persuasion to avoid solemnizing the marriage till he arrived.

The cheeping of the bird reached her ears again. Rajula

drew the curtain aside just a small chink and peered out of her palanquin cautiously. Luckily, Rikhyepal had ridden ahead.

'Don't grieve, girl,' she heard the bird say. 'It's no use. But I can well understand how you feel, because I'm unhappy too.'

Rajula stared at the bird. 'O bird, can you really speak?' she asked. 'How did you guess that I'm miserable? But you've revived my hopes, and I can't tell you how grateful I am. How do you manage to survive in this frozen waste? Also . . . can I ask why you are so unhappy?'

'I'm accursed,' said the bird. A sound like a tiny sob tore out of its throat. 'A whimsical sorcerer once granted me the gift of speech. But by chance I witnessed a secret rite he was performing. Afraid I might share the knowledge with others, he condemned me to live here, far from human habitation. If I fly to a warmer place, my head will burst. Oh, how I long for the green valleys I lived in once, the crisp golden grain and the luscious fruit I devoured so greedily! I begged him to take back his curse. He wouldn't, but he granted me the power of prophecy as a sop. So I amuse myself by throwing titbits of their future to people who pass by. Some are pleased to find out, some not.'

'Is it true that I will not marry Rikhyepal?' Rajula began eagerly when she heard shouts again.

'That evil bird! I'll shut it up, once and for all!' Rikhyepal had returned, probably to check on her.

Rajula cowered inside her palanquin as his horse thundered by. She prayed with all her heart that the bird would remain safe. There was so much she wanted to ask it. But would she find the opportunity again? Who knew . . .

Throughout the journey, hope bobbed up and down in Rajula's heart like a frail boat tossed by the waves. She clung to it even when she reached the palace where she was to live.

A magnificent building. Two gilded lions guarded the entrance, which was manned by fur-clad guards wielding large spears. Inside, the ceiling was highly ornamented and painted with bright colours. Shimmering brocade hangings decorated the walls. To her amazement, each and every luxury she could think of was available. She was provided a silver-framed bed to sleep upon, covered with luxurious satin quilts and the finest silk carpets to tread on. But it could never match Malushahi's palace.

News of her arrival soon spread. She was even more astonished when she learned that people were thronging to the palace, eager to catch a glimpse of her. They had heard that her beauty was unparalleled. Proud and elated by this response, at first, Rikhyepal made her sit on a balcony for his subjects to view her, decked in all the magnificent robes and jewellery he could provide. But as crowds continued to gather day after day, he became uneasy, even apprehensive.

'This is becoming too much,' she heard him say to his chief minister. 'People are travelling from distant parts to catch a glimpse of my bride. I fear that word of her beauty might reach the king of China. Suppose he decides to take her for himself? We will not be able to fight him off.'

'You are right, your majesty,' said the minister. 'Maybe you should keep her hidden away. And tell the priest to hurry up with the wedding date.'

Rajula was taken aback when she was suddenly made to shift to one of the innermost rooms of the palace, a room that could only be accessed by crossing seven others, all locked and guarded.

'Why are you imprisoning me like a thief or a murderer?' she cried out to Rikhyepal when he visited her there.

'I want to keep my bride safe till we get married,' he replied with an enigmatic smile.

The very next day, the same pandit, who had accompanied her from her village, arrived again.

He produced the *kangan*, the bracelet made of coloured thread, which was such an important part of the wedding rituals.

'I cannot postpone your wedding any longer, child,' he said. 'In any case you told me that you wanted to wait only until you reached here. So let me begin the ceremonies and put this auspicious bracelet on your wrist. It can only be untied by your bridegroom.'

Stunned, Rajula was unable to speak for a moment. Then she somehow gathered her wits.

'You are right, Panditjyu,' she said. 'I had requested you to wait till I reached this distant land. And you are most welcome to go ahead with the rituals. But before you begin, I would like to speak to my bridegroom in private first. Please could you ask the honourable king Rikhyepal to come here?'

The pandit gazed at her for a moment as if trying to read her mind. Then he shrugged and said, 'As you wish, child. But as your well-wisher I would like to give you a piece of advice. Do not try to put off the wedding again.'

Rajula remained silent as the priest threw a suspicious glance at her, then rose and left.

Within minutes Rikhyepal burst into the room. There was a bright smile on his face and the overpowering scent of the musk perfume he liked to use filled the room, suffocating her. Rajula shuddered inwardly.

'You sent for me?' he asked. 'What is it? Are you not comfortable here? You know I only did this to keep you safe from harm. Soon we'll be married, and there will be no need to keep you locked up.'

Rajula lowered her eyes and smiled coyly. 'There was something I wanted to say . . . It . . . it's embarrassing for a girl to confess this, but with your charming looks and gentle smile, you have won a place in my heart. There is nothing I would like better than to become your queen as soon as possible.'

'So do I! I've been longing to make you my wife since the day I set eyes on you!' Rikhyepal's eyes glittered as he said this.

Rajula suddenly turned serious. 'There is only one problem . . .'

'A problem?' His smile was wiped out at once. He narrowed his eyes to examine her face. His voice was hard as he said, 'I consulted the priest and he is sure that the auspicious time has come.'

'Alas, he does not know that a terrible illness will strike any man who marries me any time in the next seven years. I'm afraid . . . my father did not give him the right horoscope to check. I can't hide this any longer . . . I-I don't want anything bad to happen to you. We will have to wait. Please, please promise that you will treat me like a sister for the next seven years. After that we can get married safely.'

Rikhyepal's face flushed with rage. 'Seven years? What are you talking about? I did not bring you here to make you my sister! Is this a ploy? I have heard the king of Katyur wanted to marry you!'

Rajula folded her hands and went down on her knees. 'Do you really believe the king of Katyur would cross the high mountains to come between us now? It is only for your welfare, believe me. Please promise me you'll agree!' she pleaded.

Rikhyepal sighed deeply, then chewed his lip, confounded by this revelation. His brow furrowed and his eyes probed her face, as if trying to guess if she spoke the truth. Rajula trembled inside. She forced herself to look so downcast that he could not believe she was up to any trickery. He sighed again.

'I cannot send you back now,' he said, 'though I would dearly like to, just to punish your father for his deceit. But how will I explain it to my people? The shame of it . . . to bring you here with so much pomp . . . for nothing!'

He turned and paced the room, then raised a threatening finger and said, 'But remember, you cannot back out after this. And . . .' his voice hardened, 'you will remain here in this room all the time. Each and every moment.'

Rajula's voice could barely be heard as she whispered, 'I accept, honoured king, I accept your terms.'

21

Where Is Rajula?

Malushahi could not wait to find Rajula and bring her home as his bride.

He knew, however, that they had to be even more careful than last time. 'Respected Mamjyu, you are absolutely right,' he said. 'We must change form—camouflage ourselves so effectively that no one can have the slightest inkling who we are. But let us not waste time. Even a moment's delay could be disastrous.'

'I agree, son,' Mrityunjaya nodded. 'We must set off as soon as we can.'

He bowed to Guru Khekidas. 'Honoured Gurujyu, we need disguises that would fool the most wily,' he said. 'I myself am well versed in the art of magic, as you all know. But we are faced with a formidable foe. One man's knowledge may not prove equal to the task. If we put all our heads together, we should be able to come up with a foolproof plan.'

'We can definitely do that,' said the guru, beckoning the other magicians. 'What do you say, my friends? We have spent so many years poring over the ancient books, and learnt and practised numerous methods of transformation. We have the power to turn ourselves into birds and beasts, rocks and trees; we even know how to merge into the air and disappear from sight.'

'Of course, Gurujyu!' A young magician jumped up, gesturing wildly. Numerous rings studded with different coloured stones flashed on his fingers. 'It will be child's play for us to create disguises that even Sunapati will not be able to see through—no matter how great his powers are rumoured to be. This is a challenge to our skills and we will meet it!' He shook his fist to show he meant what he was saying.

'Pardon my discourtesy, Gurujyu, but whatever you do, pleased do it quickly!' Malushahi broke in, cracking his knuckles impatiently. 'And this time we must not fail!'

Somewhat flustered at having their grand speeches interrupted, the sorcerers hurriedly opened up their gold-embroidered bags of charms and began to rifle through them, while Malushahi paced up and down, his brow taut with irritation.

After a while, Guru Khekidas approached him. 'We have come up with a good plan, Maharaj. Let all the men assemble, we're ready to begin.'

A quick command brought all the soldiers running to the spot. And as Malushahi's army stood before them in rows, Khekidas and the other sorcerers began to chant their spells.

The effect was startling. Gasps, guffaws and shrill chirps arose as a flock of brown, yellow-beaked mynahs was found occupying the two front rows. Even as the men behind them were exclaiming at the sound of human speech emerging from the birds' mouths, they were transformed, too, into glossy black crows. A flock of spotted monal pheasants followed the crows, their magnificent green breasts glistening in the sun. Animal forms were next. They took a little more time as a brief argument arose among the sorcerers. But it was soon resolved and little by little, some laughing, some gesturing, some turning tail with fright—the remaining soldiers abandoned their human forms to turn into monkeys, goats and rabbits.

Mrityunjaya himself tied a magic root around Malushahi's neck and turned him into a brilliant green parrot with a curved beak as red as a rhododendron flower. He placed another root in his mouth. 'When you find Rajula,' he said, 'you can use this to change her into a parrot, too, and so escape.' Mrityunjaya assumed the guise of a huge griffon vulture, native to Tibet, while the guru chose to become a musk deer.

While the magicians were following suit, Malushahi flew up to the branch of a tree to address the men. 'Last time we fell into a trap,' he said, 'so we need to be extra careful. We may not be recognizable as humans, still you must stay close to dense bushes and thick foliage as we travel to Rajula's village. Shall we set off?'

'Yes, Maharaj!' The words sounded strange, coming from the motley crowd of birds and animals.

The extraordinary army moved on again. In a short while they reached the outskirts of Rajula's village.

'I will go and scout around first,' Malushahi announced. 'Remember—do not show yourselves to anyone.'

Malushahi flew swiftly to Rajula's home. After circling it a few times and failing to make sense of the sounds coming from inside, he perched on a tree outside. Was it her mother? His wings quivered with excitement.

Ganguli was seated on the low wall that ran around the stone-paved courtyard, with a *thali* of uncooked rice in her lap. She was making attempts to pick out stones from it, but Malushahi could see that she was unable to concentrate. She would sigh now and again, pause and turn to gaze at the mountains that lay to the north. A peculiar apprehension knotted Malushahi's belly. Why was she so distracted and downcast?

His fear escalated when Sunapati strode out of the house. He looked the way he always did—confident and in full control.

'When will you give up moping, Rajula's mother,' he said brusquely. 'She's gone now, the way all daughters have to go one day when they get married and leave their parents' home.'

Malushahi almost fell out of the tree when he heard that. He was so stunned that he barely caught Ganguli's reply.

'She did not need to go so far,' Rajula's mother was saying. 'And I don't know how you could let your daughter go over the mountains without getting her married properly. If the pandit said the time was not auspicious, you could have postponed the wedding.'

These words shocked Malushahi even more, confused him, but brought a wisp of hope fluttering back into his heart.

'And turned the bridegroom back? Worse still, run the risk of having that no-good Malushahi constantly chasing her, trying to lure her away? Rikhyepal is a man of honour, Ganguli, unlike the king of Katyur. Who knows, our Raju might be a married woman already.'

'We should have gone with her . . . at least seen our daughter's wedding,' Ganguli wiped her eyes.

'And you would have able to make that journey? Do you know how hard it is to cross the high mountains? Apart from the cold, the very air gets squeezed out of your chest.' Sunapati glowered.

'Ah . . . you should have let her marry Malushahi. She's our only child. We could have set eyes on her beloved face now and again.'

'You are a foolish woman! Did he approach me like

a respectable man and offer to marry her?' Sunapati thundered and stomped off.

Malushahi's head was whirling. Rajula in Tibet! And not married yet! The gods had favoured him. But this did not mean that he could wait for them to drop Rajula into his arms—the way it had seemed to happen the first time they met. The ease of their first encounter had misled them, made them feel that nothing would come in their way. How different it had turned out to be! But he could not afford to linger. He had learnt enough. He zipped through the air to the camping spot and informed his uncle about all he had heard.

'How astonishing! Imagine sending her off like that!' Mrityunjaya exclaimed. 'But it means all is not lost. Only, we have to brace ourselves for a far more taxing journey. However, we are equal to it. Aren't we, my men?'

'Indeed we are! Yes, we are!' shouted the troops in one voice.

Within minutes members of the assorted battalion were scampering up the steep slopes on the path that led to Tibet, some winging through the increasingly chilly air. It took a few days of the most arduous trekking to reach the snowbound passes that led through the Himalayas.

They were labouring over them, when they got a surprise.

The snowbird.

'What are you doing here? Where are you off to, my friends?' it cheeped. 'You are inhabitants of the lower reaches. Don't you fear for your lives in this dangerous place?'

'We are on a mission,' Malushahi replied, 'and as brave warriors we consider our lives of no consequence. We are going to rescue a girl.'

'A girl? Ah-h, are you talking about that charming maiden, pale with sorrow, tears trembling on her cheeks like a shower of pearls, who crossed these passes just a week ago? Hurry on, then, and good luck to you! My powers of prophecy tell me she is not meant for Rikhyepal. But who knows what her fate might be if he is thwarted?'

'You saw Rajula? Oh wondrous bird, how can I thank you!' Malushahi dipped his parrot head to the snowbird. 'You have kept hope alive in my heart! If there's anything I can ever do for you, please let me know. Now, my good men, let us speed our steps and in next to no time we'll reach our destination.'

Malushahi's strange army pressed on so determinedly that soon they had reached the borders of Rikhyepal's kingdom. After halting to rest and forage for food, they set off for the capital city. That's where they expected to find Rajula. The soldiers in the form of monkeys and birds acted as scouts and spies, picking up bits of information from travellers at wayside inns and on the highways. When they were quite close, Malushahi insisted they go on through the night, so as not to waste any time getting there.

22

On the Trail

Dawn was breaking when they reached the outskirts of the city. 'Let us halt here,' Mrityunjaya said. His head bobbed as he flew down to the ground.

'Yes, indeed. So many animals and birds grouped together will surely arouse suspicion.' Guru Khekidas twitched his ears as he glanced around cautiously.

'I'll go ahead,' Malushahi said, 'while you all rest here. The way I did at her village. A single parrot will not be noticeable. I'll find her and bring her back.'

'Malu, my son, we have to act with great caution,' said Mrityunjaya Singh gently. 'The first thing to do, of course, is to discover where she is being held. But I suggest we send a few monkeys to spy before you go and fetch Rajula.'

'I want to go myself,' Malushahi insisted. 'I have come all this way to find her. I can't bear to wait any longer!'

'Listen to your uncle's suggestion, son,' Guru Kekhidas intervened. 'He is giving sound advice. You should save your energy for the rescue because you are the only one who can do it. Rajula may not agree to come with anyone else.'

'That she won't!' Malushahi proclaimed. He continued with a deep sigh, 'Oh . . . it's impossible for me to be so near and have to wait to meet her.'

'You will, very soon,' his uncle said. 'But remember, no one must get the slightest inkling that we are here to take Rajula back. We don't want Rikhyepal to attack before we have found her.'

'All right, Mamjyu, Gurujyu, just as you say. I'll wait.' Malushahi let his restless wings drop.

'We will go right away.' The monkey-soldiers, who were busy picking out lice from each other's backs, started up.

'It will be a good opportunity to get proper food, too,' one flung over his shoulder as they pranced off.

The monkeys took a few hours to return, hours that felt like years to Malushahi. The moment the first scout scurried into view, Malushahi darted at him. 'So what did your discover?' he asked. 'Did you find Rajula?'

'There is not much to eat in this place,' the monkey replied as he took a bite from something in his hand, 'though I managed to snatch these dumplings. Wasn't the man enjoying them at the eating place annoyed?'

'You were always a greedy fellow,' another scolded. 'If you hadn't caused such a commotion, we wouldn't have been forced to flee, and I would have learned more.'

'You discovered enough.'

'Stop your chattering! What did you find out?' Malushahi yelled so loudly that the monkey-soldier almost dropped the dumpling he was nibbling at.

'Forgive us, your majesty,' he bowed contritely. 'I was so hungry that food was all I could think of. We have brought back some useful information. The men at the eating place were talking about the beautiful girl the king has brought back from over the mountains. They were wondering why he first allowed everyone to come and admire her, then suddenly decided to lock her up in a secret room in the palace.'

'They said,' continued the other monkey-soldier, 'that they had heard from one of the guards that she was hidden away so securely that seven rooms with seven locks have to be penetrated before anyone can get to her.'

'My poor Rajula! First being put on public display and then under lock and key. I must go to her right away!' Malushahi sprang into the air.

'Wait a minute, Maharaj. There's something more to tell you. The palace is right in the centre of the city,' the second monkey went on. 'It is the grandest building around, surrounded by many guards. You cannot miss it.'

Malushahi bobbed his parrot head impatiently. 'You did a good job.' Then he turned to his uncle.

'May I leave now, with your permission, respected Mamjyu and Gurujyu?'

'Go, Malu, go and rescue Rajula,' Mrityunjaya said, stroking Malushahi's head with his wing. 'Bring her back safely. Remember, this is a very complicated task. You must be as careful and as patient as a leopard stalking its prey. One false step could ruin everything. The moment you return with her, we will set off homewards.'

'I thank you for your blessings,' Malushahi bowed his head at his uncle's feet as well as Guru Kekhidas's.

He zoomed through the city and soon located the palace. Finding a door open, he entered as a flash of green. He glanced briefly at the people hurrying about. The courtiers splendidly decked out in bright satin and silk, the anxious messengers hurrying through passages, maids bent over their work. No one paid much attention to a bird flying around. The palace was huge, with numerous chambers opening into each other. In and out of these rooms he darted, but found no clue that could lead him to Rajula. Tired and dejected, he perched on a windowsill. Where could she be? How would he find her?

Be patient, his uncle had said. But how hard it was to bide his time when he knew his Rajula was locked up somewhere in this maze of rooms and he could not find any way to get to her . . . Locked up? In a blinding flash he remembered what the monkey-soldiers had said. That she was imprisoned behind seven rooms with seven locks. Why had he ignored this important piece of information?

Most of the rooms in the palace had doors that either lay ajar or swung open freely to let visitors in. He had not had any problem entering them. Nowhere had he come across a series of seven locked rooms. Was the information wrong? Just a rumour like most of the talk in eating places was? But it was the only lead he had. He had to find at least one room with a locked door, figure out a way to unlock it and then see if six other rooms lay beyond. As he winged his way through the palace again, slowly, hovering to take note of everything, he noticed a room that had a tightly shut door.

This might be the one he needed to enter. But how was he to unlock it? If only he'd thought of asking his sorcerers to teach him a spell that could unlock doors. Why, oh why had he been in such a hurry to rush off! Should he go back and ask them for one? No, he would look like an incompetent fool. Already, he had been made to look silly when Sunapati had outwitted him.

What was he to do? As he crouched within an alcove, racking his brains, a thought struck him. Surely the doors were unlocked sometimes? When they had to take Rajula food, for example. They had to keep her alive. He decided to wait for that opportunity.

His patience was rewarded. Light was beginning to dim inside the palace and servants hurrying to light the lamps placed in the alcoves in the walls when a plump woman sauntered into view. She carried a covered platter of food in one hand and a large key in the other. The moment she opened the door, Malushahi swooped in behind her.

Another locked door lay ahead. He could hear the maid grumbling under her breath. 'What need is there to lock her behind seven doors? As if she can escape! Where will she go? Even if she manages to avoid all the guards and get out of the palace, she will be easily discovered in the city. What a nuisance it is to unlock seven doors and lock them all over again!'

She was so preoccupied with her task that Malushahi slipped through each of the following doors undetected.

His bird heart leapt when the woman unlocked the seventh door and a familiar voice caressed his ears. But he was cautious enough to dive under the bed before the maid noticed him.

'Why do you bring me so much food? You know I cannot eat it all.' Rajula's voice sounded honey-sweet even when it was raised in complaint.

'You are growing pale and thin, my lady,' the woman replied brusquely. 'His majesty scolds me. It is my duty to keep you well fed. See, I've brought oranges for you . . . they've come from a far-off land, maybe your country.'

Malushahi heard a deep sigh. 'All right, just keep the food there and leave me alone. I am not hungry at all right now.'

'As you say, my lady,' the maid replied shortly. She put the platter down on a table and left.

The moment he heard the door slam shut, Malushahi hopped out. Rajula was picking up an orange from the platter. She gazed at it with a strange expression on her face, turned it round and round in her hand, then placed it back.

He had to attract her attention immediately. Who knew how soon the maid would return? So he flew up and perched on the oranges.

Rajula drew back with a jerk. 'How did you get in?' she cried. 'Don't you dare peck at these oranges and spoil them, you impertinent bird. I'm saving them for my beloved Malu. I know he will come, very soon, and take me away from this wretched place.' Her tone changed as her mouth began to tremble. 'How I hope it is soon! I don't want to grow old and die here, or be compelled to marry Rikhyepal.' She looked at him speculatively and her face brightened. 'If only you could carry a message from me to my Malu. Will you, Sua, when you fly away? When I tell you who Malu is and why I long for him so, you will surely understand . . .'

Tears streamed down her cheeks as she talked about their meeting and separation. Malushahi was so overcome by emotion that he could not speak. In an attempt to console her, he flew to her and nestled in her lap. How wonderful to be so close to her again after the long separation! But he must reveal who he was, put an end to her sorrow. However, Rajula spoke before he could.

'You seem to be kind-hearted, bird,' she cried, astonished, and began to stroke his feathers gently. He was about to tell her who he was, when her hand found the root around his neck.

She started up, saying, 'Who treated you so cruelly, you poor thing? Let me remove it at once!'

She untied the root and within minutes, his feathers vanished and he stood right before her eyes as tall and handsome as ever.

Rajula's colour fled as she stared at him. 'Am I dreaming?' she whispered, putting a hand to her brow. 'Is it really you?' She might have fainted if he hadn't caught her quickly.

Now it was his turn to tell her his story. He did it quickly, leaving out the details. 'But we cannot afford to waste time, my Raju,' he murmured, when he had finished. 'We must get away as soon as we can. I have a similar root here that will change you into a parrot, too.'

'Then we must hurry. The maid will soon return for the dishes,' Rajula breathed. 'We have to fly out the moment she enters. It's our only chance today.'

Malu took out the other root, which was tucked away in a corner of his mouth. A mere wisp, it expanded as he pulled it out. He tied it around her neck while she wound the one she had removed around his. And even as they gazed each other nervously, brilliant green feathers took the place of skin, red beaks that of their human mouths. Rajula stretched out a hesitant claw, Malushahi nodded, and both crept under a table and crouched there, waiting.

It felt as if a lifetime had passed before the maid returned. The moment the door swung open, the two parrots quickly darted out!

'What was that?' the maid cried, swinging her head around. Then she threw a rapid eye around the room. 'Where's the girl?'

Fortunately, she had left the other doors unlocked so they zipped through them swiftly. But the maid was faster on her feet than they had expected, sharper-witted, too. 'Those parrots! Where did they come from?' she screamed. 'The girl's changed form!'

They had barely winged out of the seventh door when she tore after them shrieking, 'She's gone! She's gone! Catch those parrots. CATCH THOSE PARROTS!'

She created such a ruckus that all the people around abandoned whatever they were doing to run after the pair of parrots. Rajula and Malushahi flew as fast as they could, but the palace was like a maze in the darkness.

The shouts and cries reached Rikhyepal as he sat eating his nightly meal. And when he discovered what the hullaballoo was all about, his brow became as black as thunder. He started up from his chair, knocking over his silver tumbler of rice wine.

'She lied to me! She has run off with Malushahi! But she will not escape!' he thundered. 'If the Katyuris know a few spells, we know hundreds more. Call the guards, and the army as well! Shut all the doors and the gates!'

23

Flight

Soon the palace was in an uproar, with people rushing to and fro, orders being barked out, doors and windows being slammed shut.

Rikhyepal had already closed his eyes and was beginning to chant a spell. Within minutes he turned into a ferocious looking hawk with wings that stretched out six feet wide, and a cruelly curved beak. As luck would have it, by then Rajula and Malushahi had found an open door that led to a courtyard and were soaring up to fly over the palace walls.

'We've almost made it,' Malushahi was saying exultantly, when they heard a whooshing sound behind them.

Rajula cast a swift eye behind her, and her heart almost stopped when she saw the huge raptor swooping on them with menacing speed. Worse still, a whole army of hawks followed close behind. Would they make it now?

'Hurry, let's get to the camp somehow!' Malushahi called. 'We can match them in numbers there.'

He dived low into one of the streets and zigzagged in between the startled people walking there, to throw the pursuing hawks off. Rajula followed. Shouts and screams filled the air as the hawks descended, too, behind them. Their huge wings brushed people's heads and arms, crashed into awnings and water pots.

'They cannot get away!' Rajula heard a blood-curdling squawk. 'Chase them down! Faster!'

She tried not to look up and flew close to the ground. The rustling of gigantic wings almost deafened her as the army of hawks hovered above them, like a menacing black cloud chasing them.

Somehow, weaving through the streets, sometimes darting inside an open door or beneath a jutting wall, they managed to evade the enemy, maintain some distance. They were beginning to tire when they reached the outskirts of the city, where the Katyuri forces were camped.

With a sense of relief they descended. But the respite was short-lived because the hawks were nearly there, too.

'Hurry,' Malushahi squawked anxiously. 'They're right behind us!'

A swarm of birds rose into the air—mynahs, pheasants and crows, forming a wall before the hawks. The rabbits, goats and monkeys hurriedly massed on the ground below. For a few moments the hawks were confused. Then they launched themselves on the Katyuri army, attacking viciously with beak and claw.

'To the river, the river! Make for the river!' Mrityunjaya called out.

Though confused by this command, their forces swept in straggly formation towards the river that lay close by.

'Chhoo-mantar-chhoo . . .
Change us all, do!'

Khekidas in his musk deer form began to intone a magic spell even as a hawk was swooping on him. Its sharp cruel beak tore off a tuft of fur, but before it could rip his flesh, the guru slid away. He had taken the form of a fish and was plunging into the river.

All the Katyuris turned into fishes, too, as they jumped into the chilly stream. The water rippled and bubbled as they jostled each other, but the swift current bore them along southward. They tumbled over rapids, whirled in eddies, even as the army of hawks hovered above, uncertain how to assault them but unwilling to concede the battle.

The advantage could not last long, however. Once he had taken stock, Rikhyepal countered the situation with another spell, and a host of kingfishers began to dive into the water, trying to gore and kill the fish. The guru lost no time in retaliating with his own magic. Soon the fish wriggled out of the water and an army of snakes slithered onto the river banks, curling under rocks, hissing at the kingfishers that began to dart back, totally losing their momentum.

Once again Rikhyepal found a way to reply to this challenge. He changed the kingfishers into mongooses that assailed the snakes, circling around them, then nipping at them.

And so the battle raged on and on as the two armies continued to change shape after shape after shape.

'How long will this continue?' Rajula cried, unable to stand the bloodshed. 'The men are suffering all because of us.'

'Till we defeat them,' Malushahi replied.

'We have to head homeward . . . it's the wisest course!' Mrityunjaya called out to Malushahi in the midst of the melee. 'Gurujyu, which is the best form to adopt?'

'We need to turn into birds again in order to fly over the mountains. Birds that can fly long and high.'

And soon an enormous flock of snow geese hurtled through the passes like a cloud driven by a gale. Once again Rikhyepal lost no time, because giant hawks darkened the air behind them.

'You will not get them! Ever, ever, ever!' mocked the snowbird as Rikhyepal zoomed past her.

'May your head burst, foul bird!' Rikhyepal squawked.

The snow geese had dropped to the ground and long furry shapes were racing down the slopes.

'Let us hunt wolves then,' Rikhyepal yelled grimly, 'in the form of snow leopards. And we shall see who wins this one!'

A growling mass of leopards bounded after the pack of wolves that were leaping down the mountains at breakneck speed. So swift was their flight and so intent on their battle were the two armies that they did not notice when the snows gave way to green meadows and then into a densely shaded forest.

It was the same place where the two wizards Sidua and Bidua Ramol practised their craft. The howling of the wolves and the leopards' snarls clashed in their ears, startling them so that Sidua's flute fell from his hand, and Bidua's hands froze in the midst of his relentless drumming.

'What kind of battle is this?' Sidua asked. 'Wolves against snow leopards! I've never seen anything like this before.'

'They . . . they are not real animals. Can't you make out? Wait . . . can you see that she-wolf with a male by her side? Do you recognize them?' Bidua whispered.

'Yes.' Sidua lowered his eyes. 'It's the . . . the beauteous Rajula and . . . King Malushahi . . . and that's his army.'

Bidua threw him a meaningful look. 'They seem to be in trouble.'

Sidua shook his head. 'Indeed . . . the leopards seem to be gaining on them. And leopards always prevail over wolves.'

'What shall we do? We cannot watch them being torn apart in front of our eyes.'

'You are absolutely right,' Sidua said. He sighed deeply. 'That was a terrible mistake on my part. How could I have cast an eye on Rajula? Lord Baghnath himself blessed their love. I must make amends.'

He bent and picked up a large pumpkin that lay on the ground before him and flung it at Rikhyepal's army. As it split open, a dense fog emerged and enveloped them.

It took a while for the Katyuris to realize that the enemy was no longer tearing into them. They stood and watched bemused, listening to the Tibetans yell and curse as they stumbled around, bumping into rocks and trees or into each other.

'They will remain shrouded in that fog for another day and another night,' Sidua said, picking up his flute again. 'And the strains of my music will confuse them even more. You can return to your natural forms if you wish. Safely.'

'How can I thank you, O celestial musician?' Malushahi said with folded hands.

Rajula, too, bowed low in gratitude.

'Ask me to play at your wedding,' Sidua said with a smile.

24

A Story like no Other

And he did. It was a wedding like no one had ever seen, one that was talked about for decades, even centuries. Not only the people of Bairath but also those of Jalnar Desh celebrated. That's because Ganguli was able to persuade Sunapati to attend and give his blessings, which he did gladly, now that Malushahi had proved his love. Dharma Devi welcomed Rajula, too, and embraced Ganguli like a long-lost sister.

'They had to demonstrate that their love is unconquerable,' she said, as they gazed fondly at the young couple, seated on their thrones, 'no matter that they were meant for each other even before they were born. We, too, had to learn that their love was stronger than any power in the world.'

Sunapati nodded slowly. He swallowed hard and said, 'My Rajula and King Malushahi have more than shown their mettle. Wait and see, their exploits will be celebrated in song and story for a long, long time.'

Dharma Devi smiled and said, 'You are absolutely right. The court poet has already composed a ballad in their honour, which the musicians will perform now for your pleasure.'

When the last part of their adventures was being enacted, the magicians stepped in to repeat their feats. Sunapati smiled and applauded loudly. He could not help glancing at a wisp of vapour coiled around a pillar in the durbar hall. It was, however, a kind guardian spirit he had placed there to protect his daughter from harm. Little did he know that his wife Ganguli had already passed on her magic charms to Rajula as a wedding gift!

Rajula and Malushahi led a long and happy married life and had many brave and beautiful children.

The story of their adventures did become immortal and is retold even today.

{The Book Mine Gems}

Rajula
and the
Web of Danger

Extra-special pages to help you know more about the story, its characters and its times

CONTENTS

HISTORY'S MYSTERIES: WHO WROTE THE *RAJULA-MALUSHAHI*?

In which we find out where *Rajula–Malushahi* comes from and who has brought the story so far . . .

The story of *Rajula–Malushahi* comes from Kumaon, one of the two regions and administrative divisions of Uttarakhand, a mountainous state in northern India. The other division is Garhwal. Kumaon includes the districts of Almora, Bageshwar, Champawat, Nainital, Pithoragarh and Udham Singh Nagar. It is bounded on the north by Tibet, on the east by Nepal, on the south by the state of Uttar Pradesh, and on the west by the Garhwal region. The people of Kumaon are known as Kumaonis and speak the Kumaoni language.

No one knows who composed the epic ballad *Rajula–Malushahi*. It has been performed in Kumaon for about a thousand years, and passed down orally from generation to generation in the families of traditional bards.

In modern times, it was theatre person Mohan Upreti, who revived many folk traditions in Uttarakhand, and contributed greatly to keeping *Rajula–Malushahi* alive. Born in Almora in Uttarakhand in 1925, Upreti had a passion for music and theatre, and gave his debut performance while at school in Ramsay College. Later, at the University of Allahabad, he formed his own theatre group called Lok Kalakar Sangh, which was influenced by the India People's Theatre Association and the Progressive Writers' Movement, both of which brought important social and cultural issues to the people.

Even as a young man, Upreti understood the importance of folk traditions and why they must be preserved for the generations to come. In the 1940s and 50s, he travelled through the villages of Uttarakhand with the playwright B.L. Sah, carefully collecting local folk songs that were slowly disappearing from the region. Only a handful of people knew them anymore, and little or no record existed about them.

Mohan Upreti brought Kumaoni culture and music into national focus by setting up the Parvatiya Kala Kendra (Centre for Arts of the Hills) in Delhi in 1968. This organization is still active, and produces plays and ballads rooted in the culture of the region. Along with well-known theatre personality Brij Mohan Shah, who was the director of the National School of Drama, New Delhi (NSD), at the time, Upreti played a crucial role in reviving theatre in Uttarakhand. He was himself on the NSD faculty for many years, and directed plays for the NSD Repertory Company, a branch of NSD that provided a platform for its graduates. Among other works, Upreti also spent many years working to revive the traditional forms of the Ramlila and introduce it to urban audiences.

In 1980 the Sangeet Natak Akademi published his deeply researched book on the epic ballad *Rajula–Malushahi*. He also composed a musical play based on the ballad, which is often performed by the Parvatiya Kala Kendra. His book on *Rajula–Malushahi* provides its history, its place in the culture of Kumaon, and goes into detail about the storytelling and singing styles of three important bards, Mohan Singh, Jogaram and Gopidas, who were its main performers in the twentieth century and whose work he studied closely.

THE THREE BARDS

1.
NAME: Mohan Singh Rithagarhi
PROFESSION: Farmer
LIVED IN: Village Baidibagarh, P.O. Kanarichina, Rithagarh
Distt: Almora

2.
NAME: Gopidas
PROFESSION: Tailor, but belonged to a family of professional ballad singers
LIVED IN: Kausani, Distt: Almora

3.
NAME: Jogaram
PROFESSION: Ballad singer
LIVED IN: Village Patiya, Distt: Almora

SHH... DON'T TELL ANYONE !

In which we investigate top secret files on the *Rajula-Malushahi* and share them with you...

★ The epic ballad *Rajula–Malushahi* is said to have been composed around the 10th century AD. It is the story of a romance between a king and the daughter of a wealthy trader. They belonged to different communities. Since it was not a written text, as happened with much of our folklore, each storyteller added his own touch when he retold it. Even in recent times, while the main storyline remains the same, the bards who sing it have added their own details. This intriguing tale travels through different regions of Kumaon and even to Tibet in some of the versions. Magic plays an important role in the action, and makes it fun and interesting.

★ The *Rajula–Malushahi* is different in theme and story matter from other folk ballads of India, which are mostly written in praise of a legendary hero. What is special is that the heroine, a girl, Rajula takes the initiative and actually challenges her beloved Malushahi to prove himself worthy of her instead of surrendering meekly. She displays great courage and presence of mind in dealing with all the obstacles that come in her way, and never gives up. And while gods and goddesses play a role, *Rajula–Malushahi* is not religious in nature.

★ Sung by professional bards, the performance of the *Rajula–Malushahi* was often an all-day affair and could take ten to twelve hours altogether. Mohan Upreti says that its music offers the best and richest in the folk music repertoire of Kumaon. It is extremely haunting, and the presence of the imposing and beautiful Himalayas and the moods of the different seasons seem to be reflected in the melodies. No wonder the travelling bards who presented it were treated with great respect and admired highly! They provided action-packed and magical entertainment that was very welcome in the usually backbreaking routine of villagers who formed its main audience.

★ The bards presented different versions of the main storyline, varying the episodes, adding their own imagery and metaphors, and creating their own verse patterns. Descriptions of the landscape, the action and minor episodes varied according to the singer. Some used extremely poetic imagery while others concentrated on the action. And while the singer might vary his language at different performances, he would never change his musical pattern.

★ In the narration, sung verses were alternated with spoken passages, and occasionally the bard would break into second person and address the character directly. A small drum or *hurka* was used to maintain the rhythmic pattern and two male voices accompanied the lead singer. At intervals they would take over, following his cue. The musical patterns of the bards varied, too, according to their creative impulses and abilities. Jogaram, for example would chant the passages where magic played a role. Sometimes they would clap during the description of a long march. It was not uncommon for listeners to go into a trance during these performances and start dancing. At such points, the bard would keep repeating the episodes, varying them till the audience calmed down.

★ *Rajula–Malushahi* is sung in the Kumaoni language but can reflect the local speech of the performer. Some singers occasionally add an appropriate Hindi verse or couplet to illustrate or highlight a point.

- At the end of the performance, the singer would bless the audience, thank his patron (who would make the performance possible by paying them) and the two men who provided an accompaniment. He would also introduce himself and his associates. At the very end he would bless Rajula and Malushahi, and wish them a long and happy married life.

- Most of the traditional performers belonged to the community known as the *khasas*, who were the original inhabitants of this region. They believed they were the descendants of Lord Shiva's drummers, from the time when he lived in the Himalayas.

IN THE NEWS

In which we tell you what was happening in our country in that era. The 10th century in India was a period of turmoil. Like the Katyuris, the dynasty to which King Malushahi belonged, many powerful dynasties lost their power...

★ In 910 AD, Parantaka I of the Chola dynasty drove out the Pandyas from southern India into modern-day Sri Lanka, which he also conquered eventually. The Chola dynasty ruled over shifting territories from the 3rd century BC to the 13th century AD, and was one of the longest-ruling empires in south India.

★ Rajaraja the Great, one of the greatest emperors of the Chola dynasty, was born in 947 AD and crowned in 985 AD. Rajaraja invaded Sri Lanka in 993 AD and occupied the northern half. The following year he attacked the region now known as Kerala.

★ Tailapa II defeated his Rashtrakuta overlords and established the Western Chalukya dynasty in 973 AD.

The Rashtrakutas were a dynasty that ruled nearly all of present-day Karnataka, Maharashtra and parts of Andhra Pradesh for over two centuries.

★ The powerful Gurjara-Pratiharas who reigned in western and northern India went into a decline after attempts to fight off the Turks in the west and the Pala (rulers of modern Bengal) advances in the east weakened their strength. They lost control of what is now Rajasthan to their feudatories, and the Chandelas captured the strategic fortress of Gwalior in central India around 950 AD.

★ Rajashekhara, the eminent Sanskrit poet, dramatist, critic and court poet of the Gurjara-Pratiharas, wrote *Kavyamimamsa* sometime between 880 and 920 AD. The work is essentially a guide for poets and explains the elements of a good poem and how to compose one.

★ Pampa, an early Kannada language poet, was born in 902 AD and earned the title of Adikavi, or first poet, because of his immense contribution to Kannada literature. He became famous for his *Adipurana*

(941 AD), the life history of the first Jain Tirthankara, Rishabhadeva. Pampa's other notable work was *Vikramarjuna Vijaya*, the author's version of the *Mahabharata*, with Arjuna as the hero. Also known as the *Pampa Bharata*, it is written in praise of his patron, King Chalukya Arikeseri of Vemulavada, comparing the king with Arjuna.

★ Sri Ponna was also a famous Kannada poet in the court of Rashtrakuta king Krishna III (939–968 AD). The ruler bestowed two titles on him—*Kavi Chakravarti* or 'emperor of poets' and *Ubhayakavi Chakravarti* or 'imperial poet in two languages' for his mastery of Sanskrit as well as Kannada. Ponna is often considered one of the *Ratnatraya* or 'three gems of Kannada literature'—Adikavi Pampa and Ranna being the other two.

★ Ranna, the third gem, was born in 949 AD in Muduvolalu (Mudhol, Karnataka). His ancestors were from the Jain Balegara community of bangle-sellers. He began to study Sanskrit, Prakrit and Kannada at an early age from the learned Ajitsenacharya. Ranna was attached to the court of King Tailapa II and his successor King Satyashraya of the Western Chalukya empire. His famous work *Gada Yuddha* was written in 982 AD in which he narrated the story of the duel with maces (*gada*) between Bhima and Duryodhana. Ranna compared his patron king Satyashraya to Bhima. He was rewarded with the title of *Kavi Chakravarti* (emperor of poets). He wrote in Halegannada, which was an older version of the Kannada language. *Rannakanda*, the oldest still existing dictionary in Kannada, is among his four major literary works, three of which are still available.

★ The famous Iron Pillar near the Qutub Minar, it is said, was moved to Delhi during the 10th century. The emperor Chandragupta Vikramaditya of the Gupta dynasty (375–414 AD) had erected it at a place called Vishnupadagiri (meaning 'hill with footprint of Lord Vishnu') identified as Udayagiri in the vicinity of Vidisha, Madhya Pradesh. Vishnupadagiri lies on the Tropic of Cancer and was an important centre of astronomical studies during the Gupta period. The Iron Pillar apparently served as a sundial in its original location. One of the rulers of the Tomar dynasty, a Rajput clan, transported it to Delhi.

★ The Chandela dynasty, originally vassals of the Gurjara-Pratihara kings, became powerful in their own right in central India at this time and began to build the famous temples in Khajuraho from 950 to 1150 AD. Khajuraho is located in Madhya Pradesh at a distance of 620 kilometres south-east of Delhi. There were originally over 80 temples, of which only 25 now stand in a reasonable state of preservation, scattered over an area of about 20 square kilometres. A UNESCO World Heritage site, they are considered an architectural marvel and Khajuraho is a major tourist destination.

★ The Chand Baori, a vast well with flights of steps on three sides, was constructed in Abhaneri in the 10th century. This is a small town 95 kilometres from Jaipur, famous for its stepwells. The enormous well has the dimensions of a seven-storey building and is decorated with delicate carvings—truly an extraordinary feat of architecture. It is 35 metres deep and water can be drawn from any level. The popular Harshat Mata temple is situated opposite the well. The name Abhaneri is said to be a corruption of Abha Nagari or 'bright city' and Harshat Mata is the cheerful goddess of joy.

THE STORY OF THE STORY

In which we tell you what could have inspired this story . . .

★ The origin of the ballad is unknown, but its historical period can be roughly made out through its main characters. Malushahi is described as the king of Katyur whose capital was the city of Bairath. The Katyuri kings held sway in the region from the 7th century AD to the 10th century AD. At the height of their power, Kartikeyapur (present-day Baijnath) was their capital. As their hold grew weak, their kingdom broke up into small, scattered estates. The fact that Malushahi rules in Bairath (present-day Chaukhutia) proves that the story dates from the period of their decline.

★ While it is a story about love, the narrative springs from the beliefs, the prejudices and the lifestyle of the people of that time. Kumaon is a region with varying landscape and diverse communities. The high Himalayas lie to the north and the land slopes down to forests and valleys through which the rivers that rise from Himalayan glaciers flow. Tibet lies beyond the mountain range and can only be accessed through treacherous mountain passes. The Shaukas—the race to which Rajula belongs—live in the border region between India and Tibet, described as Jalnar Desh in the story. They traded with Tibet, called Hundesh, and carried back goods to sell in the lower reaches of Kumaon. Since they were different in appearance from the other Kumaonis and interacted with the Tibetans, people were somewhat wary of them. At that time, the supernatural had a strong hold on people's minds—even the Europeans believed Tibet to be a land of mystery and magic. All sorts of theories and beliefs existed about the Shaukas' knowledge of sorcery. Great heights can create physical discomfort in those not used to them and lack of oxygen can even cause hallucinations. Perhaps this natural phenomenon is behind other people's fear of the Shaukas' magic spells and the reason why the Katyuris fear Sunapati Shauka.

★ Sunapati is described as the king of the Shaukas in some versions, a leading merchant in others. Since the Shaukas were dependent on trade for their livelihood, the idea that he would marry his daughter to a Tibetan ruler to gain commercial advantage probably seemed to make sense as the central point of conflict in the story. However, just the differences between the two cultures and communities (Rajula's and Malushahi's) were a strong enough reason for resistance to the plans of the hero and heroine of the story.

- The town of Bageshwar plays a crucial role in the story because that is where Rajula and Malushahi first meet. The great fair held in January to celebrate the festival of Makar Sankranti or Uttarayani was an occasion for people of different regions to mingle. Apart from its religious significance, it was very important for trade. Thus it lent itself easily as a setting for an encounter between the daughter of a trader and the ruler of a nearby kingdom who was attending it for religious reasons.

- The legendary musicians Sidua and Bidua Ramol with their accompanying fairies, who are part of Kumaoni folklore, were probably woven in to provide an interesting episode and an occasion for Rajula to employ her wit and use her magic. The second episode of Fachua adds humour and the third with the Mahara brothers heightens the element of danger her journey involved.

★ Kumaoni folklore is full of bird and animal stories, hence it's no surprise that birds take part in the action here, such as the raven that helps locate Malushahi, and the fascinating snowbird.

★ In some versions of the story, Rajula is engaged to two Tibetan brothers at the same time, which seems odd and creates an intriguing situation. However, the fact is, polyandry or the custom of a woman having more than one husband was not unusual in Tibet.

★ The author of this book has combined interesting episodes from the versions of the three famous bards and creates her own retelling.

FOLK BALLADS IN DIFFERENT STATES OF INDIA

In which we offer a glimpse of bardic traditions from other parts of the country . . .

★ *PABUJI KI PHAD* is the most famous folk epic in Rajasthan. It celebrates the heroism of the Rathore chief, Pabuji, who is worshipped as a folk deity and said to possess god-like powers. Nomadic folk musicians known as the Bhopas narrate it in song and illustrate the story with a *phad*—a sheet or cloth scroll on which scenes from the story are painted or sewn. These scenes are not placed in any particular order and the Bhopa will select an episode as he pleases. The *phad* is treated as a sacred object—Pabuji's temple—by the Bhopas who make daily offerings to it. People believe that the god descends on the Bhopa when he sings the ballad. The narration of the ballad follows a specific ritual. The space where it is set up is first purified and a lamp rotated around the *phad*. This lamp is also used to illuminate scenes during the storytelling, which usually takes place at night. Usually the Bhopa will tell the story and his wife hold up the lamp and repeat a few lines. Sometimes a child might dance alongside as well.

★ *PANDAVANI* is a folk ballad form native to Chhattisgarh and Bihar. As its name suggests, it is a narration of the story of the Pandavas and draws from the *Mahabharata*. Traditionally a male domain, famous women Pandavani singers like Teejan Bai have taken to it in recent times and made it popular internationally. A Pandavani group consists of a lead artist and some supporting singers and musicians. The lead artist narrates the scenes in a very dramatic manner, adopting the roles of the characters and occasionally breaking into dance. She/he uses an *ektara*, a single-stringed instrument, for rhythmic accompaniment or as a prop. For example, Teejan Bai transforms her *ektara* into Bhima's mace, Arjun's bow or Draupadi's hair. There are two styles of narration in Pandavani—the Vedamati and the Kapalik. In the Vedamati style the lead artist remains seated on the floor throughout the performance and simply tells the story. The Kapalik style is more animated and the narrator actually enacts the scenes.

★ *POVADA* is a Marathi folk ballad style that depicts the heroic deeds of great kings and is believed to have originated from Vedic literature. The *povada* is a form rather than one particular story and in contemporary times *povadas* can deal with social and political events. The ballad is composed in four to forty stanzas, each consisting of three or four lines. The earliest known *povada* hails from the 17th century when the poet Adyandas (or Agindas) was commissioned by Shivaji's mother Jijabai to commemorate his victory over Afzal Khan. It tells the story of Shivaji's encounter with Afzal Khan in 1659, which ended in the latter's death.

The lead performer wears an *angarakha* and a *churidar* with a cummerband and a turban on his head. He holds a tambourine, which he strikes from time to time. As is common in folk ballad performances, he narrates the story as well as enacts the role of the hero. His accompanists, known as *jhilkari*, play the minor characters and provide musical, vocal and instrumental support. The performance begins with a hymn invoking Lord Ganesha and the storytelling proceeds in a combination of poetry and prose. The *jhilkaris* join in or repeat certain lines, and also offer appropriate responses. The language is simple, but the rhythms are brisk and spirited. The *dholak*, *dimdi* or small drum, *daph*, and the stringed *tuntune* are the instruments used.

★ ALHA is a folk epic ballad performed in most parts of north India, in the states of Uttar Pradesh, Madhya Pradesh and Bihar by bards known as Alhets. The original *Alha Khand* was written, it is said, in the 12th century, probably by Jagnayak (or Jagnik), the court poet of the Chandela king Paramardi Deva (Parmal) who ruled in Mahoba in Bundelkhand and who features in the story. It was composed in a special metre named the *Alha*. The epic consists of a number of ballads describing the feats of two Rajput heroes, Alha and Udal (or Udani), who were the king's generals. The original manuscript has never been found and the *Alha* was handed down orally, which means that there are different versions in north Indian dialects like Bundelkhandi, Awadhi and Bhojpuri, with varying storylines.

In 1865, Englishman Charles Elliott compiled some of the versions into 23 cantos, which led to the first printed edition in 1871. The performance begins with an invocation to Goddess Bhawani and Lord Ganesh. Songs follow, which narrate episodes in the lives of the brothers, including their heroic resistance to Prithivraj Chauhan, who attacked Mahoba. The bards, always male, present it in a very dramatic manner. The *Alha* is usually sung during the monsoon season and is considered a major event in village life. The *Alha* ballads are also sung in *barats* or wedding processions to entertain the guests, as the groom makes his way to the wedding venue.

CLIMBING THE MOUNTAINS

In which we take you on a visit to some of the places Rajula and Malushahi travel through and tell you what they are like now . . .

★ Rajula was a Shauka, which means she belonged to a tribe that lives in the border regions between India and Tibet. While it is not clear which exact area the name Jalnar Desh indicates, the route described by some of the bards seems to point to the Johar valley. The picturesque town of Munsiyari lies at the entrance of this valley and was a halting point for the nomadic Shaukas on their way to Tibet and back—the others being Quithi, where they lived in winter and Milam, the last stop en route to Tibet. Situated on the banks of Goriganga River, Munsiyari is now quite popular with tourists because of its natural beauty—the fantastic view of the Himalayas, in particular Mount Panchachuli, as well as its dense forests, sparkling waterfalls and abundant opportunities for trekking. It is the base camp for the trek to the Milam glacier and other closer destinations like Khalia Top. A small museum set up by Dr. S.S. Pangtey provides a glimpse of the traditional life of the Shaukas and one can pick up local woollens and spices as well. Cultural events are organized in summer and a yearly football tournament is a huge attraction for the locals.

★ Milam lies at a height of over 11,000 feet and is accessible only by foot or on horseback even today. The river Goriganga originates here from the Milam glacier. The Shaukas lived here from June to September and this is from where their trade caravans set off for Tibet in June or July. They would travel over the high mountain passes of Unta Dhura, Jayanti Dhura and Kingribingri Dhura to the trade mart of Gyanima in Tibet, carrying rice, cotton and silk cloth, spices and jaggery on their pack animals. From Gyanima they travelled onwards to Gartok and began their return journey in late August with Tibetan wool, gold dust, borax and rock salt. After celebrating the mid-September festival of Nandashtami in their villages, the traders travelled to the plains as far as Varanasi and Kolkata to purchase silks, spices and jaggery to trade in Tibetan markets. The trade ended with the Sino-Indian War of 1962, and Milam is now a ghost village occupied by the Indo-Tibetan Border Police (ITBP).

★ Bageshwar lies on the point where the rivers Saryu, Gomti and the invisible Bhagirathi meet, and is considered a place of pilgrimage because of its connection with Lord Shiva. The temple of Baghnath, the lord of tigers, a form of Lord Shiva, was constructed in 1602, it is said, by the Chand kings, who became dominant in Kumaon after the fall of the Katyuris. This date seems to conflict with the story of Rajula and Malushahi since Rajula worshipped at the shrine. Perhaps we can allow some poetic licence, here, and who knows if an earlier temple did exist? Bageshwar is famous for the earlier mentioned fair of Uttarayani and another very popular one at Shivaratri. It also has historical and political significance. During the freedom movement, nationalist leaders would address the crowds gathered for the Uttarayani fair. The struggle against some oppressive colonial practices like *coolie begar* (forced unpaid labour) was launched here.

★ When Rajula visits Malushahi's capital Bairath, she is impressed by its magnificence. Modern- day Chaukhutia is a small town that has been identified as the Bairath of the story and the ruins of a fort constructed by the

Katyuri kings can still be viewed. The name Chaukhutia is derived from the Kumaoni word for four feet–'Chau' meaning four, and 'khut', foot. Here it indicates four paths or directions because of its location. The town is situated on the banks of the Ramganga River and is known for its excellent fishing. If you remember, Malushahi promised Rajula that she would get delicious fish to eat if she married him!

★ When Rajula encounters Fachua Doyarva with his pots of yoghurt, she guesses he must be from Doonagiri, which meant she was not too far from Bairath. Doonagiri, located 47 kilometres north of Ranikhet, has been famous for its dairy products from time immemorial. Apart from the *Rajula–Malushahi* there are folktales that mention this. According to a myth, when Hanuman was carrying the *sanjeevani booti* back to Lanka, a piece of the mountain fell here, giving this place the name Doonagiri. Myths and legends apart, Doonagiri is a beautiful spot with a spectacular view of the Himalayas. There is a temple of Vaishno Devi as well, which, however, is not as well known as the famous one in Jammu.

WHAT WOULD YOU HAVE DONE?

★ You and your husband Sunapati Shauka made a vow long ago at Chitrashila Devi's temple—to marry your daughter to Dulashahi and Dharma Devi's son. Since your daughter Rajula was born and grew up, you have not been able to approach Dharma Devi. In the meantime, your husband has betrothed Rajula to the Tibetan king, Rikhyepal. You are troubled and remind Sunapati of the vow, but he is determined to marry your daughter to the Tibetan. And then by a strange twist of fate Rajula falls in love with Malushahi, who has been visiting her in her dreams. You try to help Rajula by encouraging her to go to Bairath and tell Malushahi to come and claim her as his bride. You even help her with magic charms. But in the end, you find that despite all your efforts, your husband is still getting his way. What would you have done? Given up, or tried to find a way to get Rajula and Malushahi together?

★ You, Sidua Ramol, are captivated by Rajula's charms when you encounter her in the forest at night. Your music can mesmerize fairies, even call down the *apsaras* from Indra's court. But this ordinary human is so much in love with Malushahi that she is able to resist you and even uses magic to force you to flee. Later, you encounter Rajula and Malushahi when they are in a situation of extreme danger. The rejected Tibetan king is in hot pursuit with his army and will soon catch them. What would you have done? Joined the Tibetans as a rejected suitor, or helped Rajula and Malushahi?

★ Rajula knows that once she is married to Rikhyepal, she is lost to Malushahi. Desperate, she makes a last-ditch effort and tries to bribe you, the pandit, to prevent this from happening. She offers you a valuable ring to insist that the marriage be postponed, saying that the time is not auspicious. What would you have done? Taken the precious sapphire ring, or sympathizing with her plight, refused it and offered to help Rajula all the same?

CHARACTER CLUES-WHO AM I?

★ Rajula and I have grown up together and are the best of friends. Like her, I am engaged to be married. But my other friend Saru and I cannot help teasing her because she is betrothed to a Tibetan king, whose ways are likely to be very different. Later, when we learn that Malushahi is her true love, we help to cover up when she goes to meet him. Everything goes wrong, alas. Her father discovers what is going on and whisks her away. Later, when we return from the Uttarayani fair and try to meet our friend, her mother refuses. When we beg her to let us see Rajula for a few minutes, her father appears and gives us a good scolding. Who am I?

★ My niece comes to me with a request. She has not been blessed with children and hopes I can help her because I have all kinds of knowledge. I tell her I do not possess such powers, only a goddess can help her. But since I do not want her to go back empty handed I give her some magic charms, in case she should ever be in trouble.

These charms are of great help to her daughter Rajula later. Who am I?

★ I am a goddess with special powers. When childless women come and pray sincerely at my temple I grant their wishes and they are blessed with children. Once a strange event occurs at my temple. Two couples come to worship at the same time and the women become friends. They make a vow that they will marry the children born to them to each other, in case one is a boy and the other a girl. Unfortunately they do not keep this promise though one of the women, Ganguli, is eager to. I have to use my powers to make the young couple aware of each other. I send Malushahi to Rajula in her dreams and see that they meet later. They fall in love, and after facing many trials and tribulations, finally get married. Who am I?

★ I encounter Rajula in the forest by chance, as I am carrying pots of yoghurt to sell. The moment I see her I feel concerned that this lovely young girl is roaming around alone in this deserted place. I need a wife and it seems right that I take this poor maiden under my protection. I even agree to her ridiculous terms to prove myself a worthy suitor and do an amazing job of dancing upside down. But the sly creature tricks me and disappears mysteriously. Who am I?

★ I have two nephews, both well-built and well-to-do farmers, but they are not very clever. One day they get into a fight over a pretty girl who is discovered soaking her feet in their irrigation channel. Both are so eager to marry her that they begin to pulling her apart. As an elder, I have to intervene and tell the stupid fellows the right way to do things. They need to win the girl by preparing food that will appeal to her and ask her to choose between them. My plan would have worked if the girl had not tried to outsmart us. She got a good beating for her impertinence and lost the chance of finding a good husband. Who am I?

★ I have been cursed to live in a lonely, snowbound place and long to return to my native land. But I cannot because I know my head will burst if I do that. There is one compensating factor—I can predict the future, though not everyone is happy when I foretell them what lies ahead. One day, I see a beautiful young girl being carried to Tibet over the mountain passes. She seems in the depths of despair. Fortunately I am able to say something that brings a smile to her face, though her supposed future husband threatens me with a dagger and chases me off.

★ Dharma Devi and Malushahi both respect me greatly and come to me for advice whenever they are faced with a problem. I have all kinds of magic powers but am outwitted by the wily Sunapati Shauka. Fortunately, the king's uncle comes to my aid and rescues me along with Malushahi and his soldiers. Later, on the journey to Tibet, my magic charms play an important role in rescuing Rajula and bringing her back safely. Who am I?

ANSWERS (*in order of questions*): *Bhaguli; Ganguli's aunt; Chitrashila Devi; Fachua Dogarwa; Nagimal; the snowbird; Guru Khekidas*

MAGIC TRICKS

Magic plays an important part in Rajula and the Web of Danger. What are the different magical tricks used? Here they are in the order in which they appear.

★ SLAVE SPIRIT: Sunapati Shauka is famous for his knowledge of sorcery and feared because of it. Among the other tricks up his sleeve, he holds a spirit captive and can raise it when he needs its help. This spirit takes the form of a wisp of mist.

★ SHAPE SHIFTER: Ganguli's aunt very kindly presented her with different kinds of magical aids. One is charmed ash, which helps Rajula to take on the form of an animal in a tricky situation. All she has to do is to take a pinch of ash in her hand and repeat a spell. When she wishes to return to her normal form, she chants the spell again. Rajula uses it to escape Fachua Doryava in the form of a flea. Later, after reaching Bairath and leaving a note for the sleeping Malushahi, Rajula is in a hurry to get home and keen to avoid all the dangers that she faced during her journey to the city. She uses the charmed ash to turn into a dove and flies off.

- ★ SERPENTINE: The next charm is a gnarled and twisted root that will turn into a snake with the help of the appropriate spell. Gingerly, Rajula tucks it into her hair and finds it very useful when she has to get away from Sidua Ramol and the fairies.

- ★ MAGIC FLUTE: Sidua Ramol possesses his own brand of enchantment—the music he plays on his flute. It's so mesmerizing that not only the fairies but also the *apsaras* from Indra's court cannot resist it and begin to dance to his tune. So does Rajula. If an owl had not hooted, her journey would have ended soon after it began and she would not have reached Malushahi.

- ★ SLEEP POTION: When Rajula wants to enter Malushahi's palace unseen, she puts everyone to sleep. Does she sing an irresistible lullaby? No, she opens her silver perfume case—the one her mother gave her before she left. The attar inside it is a powerful sleep inducer—so potent that the guards, the dogs and everyone in the palace fall fast asleep. Unfortunately, the charm works so well that Rajula cannot wake Malushahi up, no matter how hard she tries! Disappointed, all she can do to inform him that she had come to meet him is leave a note.

- ★ SPY GLASS/TRACE SPELL: When Malushahi wakes up and finds out that Rajula has come and gone without meeting him, he begins to vent his disappointment loudly. Disturbed, Dharma Devi wants to track her down and summons a diviner. The old woman who comes asks for a new silver platter, pours water into it and mutters a spell. She proclaims that she can see a dove on the wing, which makes the queen mother nervous. How can Malushahi marry a girl who employs the sorcerer's art?

- ★ THE FLUTE OF GLOOM: Flutes play a big role in this story. Sidua's flute casts an enticing spell, but the flute Malushahi gets from the old bamboo in the forest plays an overpowering tune too. Only, this is a sad one, in keeping with his dejected mood. The problem is that it throws everyone else who hears it into the dumps, too. Things become so bad that the kingdom comes to a standstill and Dharma Devi is compelled to agree to his demand to go and fetch Rajula.

★ THE CALL OF THE DRUM: Malushahi is in a hurry to set off. But with all he has heard about Sunapati's powers, he needs a large army to rescue Rajula. How can he summon all the men in his kingdom at once? He may not have possessed modern forms of communication, which connect people instantly, but there was a magic drum in his guru's house. When he strikes it, all the able-bodied men in Katyur hear the sound. They abandon their work and make for the capital at once.

★ KHEKIDAS'S FIFTY-TWO SPELLS: Malushahi's army sets off, disguised as sadhus. But as they get close to Rajula's village, something in the air makes them dizzy and they fall down unconscious. Guru Khekidas revives them with the help of the fifty-two spells he has armed himself with.

★ KNOCK-OUT: It's not that easy, however, to take off with Rajula. Sunapati shrewdly guesses who these sadhus are and like, a pious man, invites them for dinner. He doctors the dessert, a delicious goat's-milk *kheer* with a potion that knocks them out for a month. That's enough time for him to try to get Rajula married to Rikhyepal and send her to Tibet.

★ DREAM-TIME: When Malushahi does not return as expected, an anxious Dharma Devi sees her son in a dream, lying pale as death in a snowy place.

★ SEEING BEYOND: Convinced that he has come to harm, she sends for her brother Mrityunjaya Singh, who is no mean magician himself. All the best sorcerers and diviners in the kingdom are sent for. As they get close to the caves where Malushahi lies unconscious with his men, a diviner can sense him close by but cannot tell the exact spot. He uses his traditional tools and throws pinches of vermilion powder and grains of rice into the air while repeating a spell. He can now see that Malushahi is inside a cave, but they still need a raven's help to get there.

★ THE SEVEN DAYS OF CHANTING: Malushahi needs to be revived, however, and it requires many powerful spells, chanted for seven days and nights. Along with the sorcerers' magic words, the king's uncle chants the Mahamrityunjaya mantra, which is said to defeat death. And the young ruler regains consciousness, along with his guru and army.

★ MASQUERADE: When they get close to Rajula's village, they realize that they need disguises that will fool even the wily Sunapati Shauka. The band of magicians summons powerful mantras that turn the men into rabbits, goats and monkeys, crows, mynahs and pheasants. Mrityunjaya himself ties a root around Malushahi's neck and transforms him into a parrot.

★ PARROT PLAY: In the form of a parrot, Malushahi makes the sad discovery that Rajula has been sent to Tibet, but is still unmarried, fortunately. The motley crew climbs the high mountains and reaches Tibet. Once they have located Rajula in the palace, the king-parrot flies there to get her out. He has another magic root tucked in his mouth. Tied around her neck, it will change her into a parrot, too, so that they can escape unnoticed.

★ RACE TO THE END: It is not so easy, however, to get away. A maid notices and sets up an outcry, and Rikhyepal, who is as well versed in magic spells, chase them with his army, transformed into hawks. A merry chase ensues, in which the Katyuris keep changing shape constantly to stay ahead of their pursuers—from animals and birds to fishes, back to birds, then wolves. The Tibetans follow suit.

★ PUMPKIN PLOY: Who wins in the end? It's a magic pumpkin that does the trick. Sidua and Bidua Ramol help Rajula and Malushahi, and their army. As the Tibetan leopards are about to pounce on the fleeing wolves, a remorseful Sidua breaks a pumpkin. A dense fog fills the air, leaving the Tibetans floundering. The others race off, all the way to Bairath and home territory.

GLOSSARY

ALU GUTAK Spicy potato dish native to Kumaon

AMA Grandmother

ANCHARIES Fairies

APSARAS Heavenly maidens who danced at the court of Indra

BABBA-HO Common expression used to indicate surprise

BADAS Disc-shaped, deep-fried snack made of lentils

BAUJYU Father; abbreviation of Babuji

DAL Lentils

GHAGHRA Voluminous ankle-length skirt worn with a blouse and *pichhaura* or head covering

GHEE Clarified butter

GHUGHUTI Spotted dove

HALWA Dessert made from semolina

HURKA Small hand-held drum

IJA Mother

JHAGULI Ankle-length dress

JHODA Kumaoni folk dance performed in a circle

KARAHI Broad, shallow cooking pot with a round base and two handles

KAKA Uncle; father's younger brother; sometimes used respectfully towards acquaintances

KAKI Aunt; Kaka's wife

KAMANDAL Container carried by mendicants to receive alms

KANGAN Here, wedding bracelet made of thread with auspicious objects tied to it, used in pre- and post-wedding rituals

KHEER Milk-based dessert often made with rice

KHICHRI A dish consisting of rice and lentils cooked together

KHOYA Milk reduced to a solid form, used to make sweets

KILMORI A purplish berry

KUNDALS Large round earrings worn by both men and women

PHAGUN Month in Hindu calendar, beginning in mid-February

MAGH Month in Hindu calendar, beginning in mid-January

MAHARAJ Term of address for a king

MAMJYU Respectful term of address for maternal uncle

MANDAP A platform where the wedding ceremony takes place

MANTRA Sounds or set of words, sacred or magical, with powers of transformation

PAAN Betel leaf

PANDIT Priest

PICHHAURA Local term for head covering or veil worn with ghaghra

PURI Deep-fried unleavened bread

RANSINGHA Curved trumpet often used to announce the arrival of kings and holy men, usually made of copper with brass trim

ROTIS Flat round unleavened bread

SAAG Leafy vegetables like spinach and mustard greens

SABZI Vegetables; here cooked into a spicy dish

SADHU Wandering ascetic; holy man who has renounced the world

SATTU Roasted barley flour

SUA Kumaoni term for parrot

SUPARI Betel nut

THALI Large metal plate

TURI Wind instrument

VAIDYA Doctor practising the ayurvedic form of medicine

REVIEW THE BOOK

In which you decide how much you liked this book . . .

★ You have just finished reading *Rajula and the Web of Danger*, a retelling of the epic ballad *Rajula–Malushahi*. Most folk epics focus on the heroic and noble deeds of great kings and warriors, but this story is a romance that highlights the bravery of a girl. Do you find the character of Rajula inspiring and why?

★ Which part of the book was more engrossing—Rajula's eventful journey to Bairath or the story of her rescue?

★ This story may seem removed from real life, but do you feel that some characters behave like people would in real-life situations? Which ones?

★ There are many tricky situations in this book and Rajula has to outwit several people to save herself. Tell us if any of the characters she fooled aroused your sympathy and why.

★ Magic plays an important role in this story. Did it add to your enjoyment of the story? Which spell or charm would you like to have?

★ If you had written *Rajula–Malushahi*, would you have done it differently? What parts would you have changed and what would you have left alone?

How do you rate this book?
Rate out of 10 stars.

★ ★ ★ ★ ★ ★ ★ ★ ★ ★

AUTHOR'S NOTE

The *Rajula–Malushahi* has been performed in Kumaon for centuries and is perhaps the most important epic ballad of the region. I learnt about it only in my late teens. Fascinated by the story, I searched for a print version without success. Years later, when I heard that the Parvatiya Kala Kendra was performing it in Delhi, I seized the opportunity to attend it along with my family. The experience whetted my curiosity further. As luck would have it, I chanced upon the Hindi novel *Rajula–Malushahi* by Gopal Upadhyaya, published by Samayik Prakshan, at a book fair and read it with great interest. Yet, something prodded me to hunt further.

Then, a few years ago, on a visit to Munsiyari, I discovered Dr. S.S. Pangtey's extensive analysis of the various retellings of this popular ballad, both oral and written, titled *Rajula–Malushahi Prem Gatha* (The Romantic Epic Rajula-Malushahi) published by Tribal Heritage Museum, Munsiyari, which provided insights into its different aspects, social, cultural and political. However, without exploring the legendary Mohan Upreti's involvement with the ballad my quest would have remained incomplete. It was only when I studied his deeply researched *Rajula–Malushahi*, published by the Sangeet Natak Akademi did I feel I had reached the core of this captivating tale.

Apart from the authors who contributed to my version of this enthralling narrative, I would like to acknowledge my indebtedness to my cousin the late Jaya Gupta, who first introduced me to the ballad. My husband Dilip supported me through this venture in ways too many to describe. Heartfelt thanks, too, to my editor and old friend Vatsala Kaul Banerjee whose inputs and suggestions were invaluable in helping *Rajula and the Web of Danger* to acquire its final shape. It was extremely kind of Prasoon Joshi to spare the time to write the introduction despite his hectic schedule, and I am immensely grateful to him.